50p

Young **Writers**

2004 POETRY COMPETITION

ONCE UPON A RHYME

IMAGINATION FOR A NEW GENERATION

Southern Counties Vol II

Edited by

GW00696076

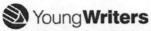 Young**Writers**

First published in Great Britain in 2004 by:
Young Writers
Remus House
Coltsfoot Drive
Peterborough
PE2 9JX
Telephone: 01733 890066
Website: www.youngwriters.co.uk

SB ISBN 1 84460 606 6

Foreword

Young Writers was established in 1991 and has been passionately devoted to the promotion of reading and writing in children and young adults ever since. The quest continues today. Young Writers remains as committed to engendering the fostering of burgeoning poetic and literary talent as ever.

This year's Young Writers competition has proven as vibrant and dynamic as ever and we are delighted to present a showcase of the best poetry from across the UK. Each poem has been carefully selected from a wealth of *Once Upon A Rhyme* entries before ultimately being published in this, our twelfth primary school poetry series.

Once again, we have been supremely impressed by the overall high quality of the entries we have received. The imagination, energy and creativity which has gone into each young writer's entry made choosing the best poems a challenging and often difficult but ultimately hugely rewarding task - the general high standard of the work submitted amply vindicating this opportunity to bring their poetry to a larger appreciative audience.

We sincerely hope you are pleased with our final selection and that you will enjoy *Once Upon A Rhyme Southern Counties Vol II* for many years to come.

Contents

Canterbury Road Primary School, Sittingbourne

Churchfields Primary School, Beckenham

Stacey Louise Brooker (11) 36
Andrew Gerrans (11) 36
Rhoni Louise Allen (11) 37
Joe Williamson-Hicks (11) 37
Rosie Stocking (10) 38
Sarah Rose Kenny (11) 38
Martin Parry (11) 38
Laura Walton (11) 39
Jack Featherstone (11) 40
Jackson Packer (10) 40
Rebecca Baker (11) 41
Samantha Offen (11) 41
Elizabeth Irene Rae (11) 42
Lily Watkins (11) 42
Joshua Bysh (10) 43
Sean Michael Williams Carmody (10) 43
George Davis (11) 44
Kele Onuoha (10) 44
Kayleigh Brotherwood (10) 45
Hannah MacLennan (11) 45
Robia Brown (11) 46

Holy Family Primary School, Addlestone

Jamie Russell (10) 47
Alice Smith (10) 48

Homefield Preparatory School, Sutton

Rowan Brearley (10) 49
Jordan Brown (9) 50
Haroon Taylor (9) 50
Louis Pickard (9) 51
Maximillian Gorynski (10) 51
Ryan Drucker (11) 52
Joshan Chana (9) 52
Murtaza Hussain (11) 53
Harry Ledger (10) 53
Timothy Hu (11) 54
Richard Mortimer (10) 55
James Peattie (11) 56
Robbie Macdonald (9) 57

Harjas S Shinmar (10)	57
Patrick Souberbielle (9)	57
Guy Aldous (11)	58
Luke Sumner (10)	58
Bradley Pfeifer (11)	59
Daniel Aldham (11)	59
Nicholas Cleeve (11)	60
Sam Chamberlain (11)	60
James Forbes (11)	61
George Cunliffe (11)	61
Christopher Everest (10)	62
Timothy Eales (11)	62
William Gonsalves (11)	63
Felix Greenhalgh (11)	63
Jaspal Chana (11)	64
Jamie Falconer (11)	64
Simon Rodin (11)	65
Harry Gunn (11)	65
James Stockwell (11)	66
Jack Ledger (11)	66
Oliver Duffy (11)	67

Hook Lane Primary School, Welling

Laura Gillham (11)	67
Harry Pieske (11)	68
Lewis Perkins (11)	68
Grace Lacey (10)	68
Alice Hunt (10)	69
Emma Budgen (11)	69
Suzanna Wilkinson (11)	69
Emma Clarkson (11)	70
Holly Baker (11)	70
Emily Kirk (11)	71
Ellie Ganney (11)	71
Rachel Jones (11)	72
Charlotte Flack (11)	72
Sean Delaney (10)	73
Jamie Hutchinson (11)	73
Harry Smith (9)	74
Michael Carr (10)	74
Isabelle Flaherty (11)	75

Sarah Powell (11)   75
Kim Stringman (11)   76
Zoe Ford (11)   76
Tom Luff (10)   77
Katie Simons & Emma Ray (9)   77
Chelsie Keeffe (9)   78
Maddison Hoyle (8)   78
Ashley Merredew (9)   78
George Bradford (9)   79
Jamie Barnes (9)   79
Thomas Barrett (9)   79

Kingscroft Junior School, Staines
Megan Bardini (9)   80
Paige Adams (9)   80
Simon Green (10)   81
Michael Brown (10)   81
Jason Cheung (10)   82
Kerry Hunter (10)   82
Rosy Lord (9)   83
Carol-Anne Coop (10)   83
Abigail Musk (9)   84
Dominic Galvin (9)   84
Jack Reeder (9)   85
Lauren Hume (10)   85
Rebecca Manning (9)   86
Chloe Poole (9)   86
Sapphire Meacock (10)   86
Kelly Smith (9)   87
Amber Dickens (10)   87
Billy Rendell (9)   87
Connie Stevens (9)   88
Joanna Sutton (9)   88
Jacob Smith (9)   89
Sophie Tanner (10)   89

Meath Green Junior School, Horley
Isobel Newbury (9)   89
Sophie Buxton (9)   90
Dean Primmer (8)   90
Elizabeth Cain (11)   91

Cherish Thorpe (8)	91
Eden Medcalf (10)	92
Callan Howard (10)	92
Kimberley Allen (11)	93
Rebecca Connor (9)	93
Laura Tadman (10)	94
Cameron May (7)	94
Rebecca Inman (9)	95
Jack Kidd (9)	95
Liberty Hill (9)	96
David Fletcher (10)	96
Callum Ross-Freeman (10)	97
Catherine Fuller (9)	97
Esther Nye (9)	98
Ben Tadman (11)	99

Minster CE Primary School, Ramsgate

Tiffany Marshall (9)	100
Jessica McDougall (8)	101
Toby Allen (9)	102
Lauren Peall (8)	103
Abby Wilkinson (9)	104
Chloe Bennett (9)	105
Lauren Hockey (9)	106
Ashley Hill (9)	107
Ellen Holland (9)	108
Hannah Jackson (9)	109

St James The Great Primary School, Thornton Heath

Albertina Marfo-Mensah (10)	110
Catherine Onoselase (10)	110
Rosalind de Souza (9)	111
Patsy Dixon (9)	111
Hannah Stock (9)	112
Denice Koduah (11)	112
Kristina Lucia (8)	113
Danielle D'Cruz (8)	113
Joanna D'Cruz (11)	114
Kathleen Lissenburg (9)	114
Sara Corvaglia (8)	115

St Stephen's Primary School, Welling

South Farnham Junior School, Farnham

Thames Ditton Junior School, Thames Ditton

Georgia Dawson (10)	138
Georgia Imrie (8)	138
Sam Ridsdale (11)	139
Dolores Honey (8)	139
Sam Carvalho (11)	140
Hannah Mitchell (8)	140
Hannah Morris	141
Cassie McCrone (8)	141
Katie Channer (11)	142
Stephen Monaghan (8)	142
Amy Davies (10)	143
Emily Hale (7)	143
Afshin Zainy (11)	144
Emily Ford (7)	144
Charlie Takhar (11)	145
Andrew Moore (7)	145
Tim Ellis (11)	146
Patrick Waters (8)	146
Julia Onken (11)	147
Emily White (11)	147
Ross Bedding (11)	148
Nicholas Dossett (11)	148
Lara Nicholls (11)	149
Edward Leithead-Docherty (11)	149
Sarah Kirby (11)	150
Oliver Roche (11)	150
Claire Gibson (10)	151
Joel Rust (10)	151
Seren Bresner (10)	152
Siobhan Byrne (11)	152
Geraint Thomas (11)	153
Jonathan Spence-Bell (10)	153
Anthony Ford (12)	154
Georgia Hallpike (11)	154
Charlie Graovac (11)	154
Alex MacIntrye (10)	155
Jack Sheppard (8)	155
Katherine Andrews (7)	155
Italy Wackrill (8)	156
Maisie Nicholls (7)	156

The Granville School, Sevenoaks

The Poems

If I Could Disappear . . .

Wouldn't it be queer
If I could disappear
And then reappear
Run with the deer
Fly without fear
With gulls on the pier.
Explore every frontier
There and here
With none to interfere
As in space I steer
Like a supersonic spear
And overhear
Of plans that domineer
This celestial sphere.
And if I'd persevere
In this pursuit premier
Then how crystal clear
Is my choice of career.
Aerospace engineer
Army Brigadier
With gadgets and gear.
Police volunteer
Invisible cashier
A magic puppeteer!
Or could I just adhere
To the precious tear
Of the prayer sincere
Or be a souvenir
That could bring some cheer
To those far and near
Whose pain is severe
All through the year.
But think what, Mum dear
Would comment if she'd hear
Of my ideas revere
She'd say, pulling my ear
'My little girl's a mere
Imagineer!'

Alysha Bhatti (9)

Christmas

You can see the Christmas lights appear,
As Santa Claus draws near.
In his sack are lots of toys,
For all those good little girls and boys.
Stockings at the end of beds,
As children rest their little heads.
All the bad things they've done that year,
Come back, with dread and fear.
That they might not get their presents and sweets
And miss out on all the treats.
But when the day is finally there,
They wake up early, but do they care?
No, because all that matters,
Is their presents and Christmas crackers.
But don't get me wrong, Christmas is that,
It's not about presents and a Santa hat.
It's about joy and giving to others
And the smiles you share with your sisters and brothers.
So remember what I've told you and you too can give out joy,
For happiness with others, is better than any toy.

Emily Zaborski (12)

The War

Cannons fired into the air,
People crying with despair.
Soldiers screaming, being shot,
Run and hide before they kill the lot.

I am a soldier on the run,
If I don't get out soon, my life will be done.
I am stored away on a truck,
I can't believe all my bad luck.

I have escaped from the awful war,
From all the blood, guts and gore.
Most of my friends are already dead,
Dear old Tim was shot in the head.

Years have gone by,
But I still cry.
The old cuts are still sore,
When I think about the Great War.

Liam Cripps (8)

My Brother, Your Brother

My brother's taller than your brother,
Yes, he's taller than yours,
If he grows anymore, he won't fit in the world,
He'll have to live in space.

Yes but, my brother's stronger than your brother,
My brother's stronger, yes?
He's stronger than your brother will ever be
Even when they're eighty.

My brother hates your brother,
Yes, so does mine,
I hate my brother,
Yes, so do I!

Lydia Snow (9)
Cage Green Primary School, Tonbridge

My Brother, Your Brother

My brother is taller than yours,
Yes, my brother is taller all right,
If he grows anymore, he won't fit through the door,
He'll have to stay outside all night.

Ah but, my brother is stronger than yours,
My brother is stronger, OK?
The more he eats, he'll get more strength,
He won't be able to stay.

Yes but, my brother can dance,
Yes, he would dance all night if he could,
He'll go to all the nightclubs,
He would stay there all night, he would.

But my brother is smarter than yours,
Yes, my brother is smarter, all right,
He knows his times tables off by heart,
He learns them day and night.

Well, I say our brothers are alike,
Yes, they support the same teams,
They like the Fast Food Rockers too,
It makes them want to scream.

Emma Wadey (10)
Cage Green Primary School, Tonbridge

Disgusting Dinner Times!

D is for the disgusting smell of the dinners
I is for the icky, sticky chairs you can't get out of
N is for the naughty, shouting children that don't eat their dinners
N is for nasty squelch of the jiggling jelly
E is for Emily slurping up her noodles
R is for the rumbling bellies that are soon going to be sick!

Abigail Newlands (8)
Cage Green Primary School, Tonbridge

Green Emerald Grass Being Thrown By A Bully

Green emerald grass being thrown by a bully,
He's pulling hair, person by person,
He's making a move for me,
I'd better run or he is going to beat me up.

He is making fun of Hugh Christie,
He's throwing stones at them,
For when it comes to being horrible,
He doesn't care.

Everyone is running because he's gonna beat them up!
When he comes near me, he says, 'What's up?'

The bell is ringing, the boy is still beating,
He is going to the teacher,
He has got expelled,
He's not happy!

Sam Balcombe (8)
Cage Green Primary School, Tonbridge

Information

I nformation is fun
N annies and grandads are full of information
F ootball information is good
O ur information is in our brains
R otting brains mean you're dumb
M en are sometimes smarter than women
A nts are quite intelligent
T empers lose control and for a split second are dim
I ntelligent people are sometimes nerds
O ur computers are good, but are bad too
N erds are very, very smart.

Frankie Fuller (8)
Cage Green Primary School, Tonbridge

Work, Work, Work!

Work, work, work!
That's all you do,
Writing in a notebook,
Is boring too.

Geography is boring
With Mrs Turk
All she does
Is be a jerk.

Music, music what do you do?
Boring music is boring with you.

Seeing your mum is the best thing of all
Oh yes, getting out of school.

Freddy Barratt (7)
Cage Green Primary School, Tonbridge

Ghost School

G hosts walking about
H ear them dripping with the blood
O h no! Don't shout
S tepping through the hallway
T ime to eat burnt wood

S hout now, no?
C oming the evil ghost
H umming along his old song
O h he is looking to eat me
O h what a lucky chance, he missed me
L ook out where ever you go, you never know who's creeping up!

Matthew Jenner (8)
Cage Green Primary School, Tonbridge

Maggie And The Dinosaur

At last they were out in the open,
Out in the shining sun.
Maggie started to look around
And saw a delicious bun.

They headed for McDonalds,
And fed the ducks on the way!
They realised they had no money,
And knew they had to pay.

Off they went to the park,
Maggie saw the swings,
Dino got overexcited
And wished he had fluttery wings.

They left the park and headed home,
And carefully crossed the road.
They were just about to open the door,
When they trod on a small, slimy toad.

Andrew Coulter (10)
Cage Green Primary School, Tonbridge

Mealtimes

M ealtimes are cool
E at a lot of healthy food
A ll the food you like is lurking in the lunch room
L eave your food, not enough
T ouch my food and you're dead
I have a packed lunch so I am safe
M ealtimes are safe when you have a packed lunch
E ggs have gone off middles
S o always have a packed lunch.

Jessica Tompsett (8)
Cage Green Primary School, Tonbridge

Best Friends!

Me and my best friend,
Always play with each other,
We invite our best friend round our house,
We even know each other's mother.

Brown hair, brown eyes,
Lots of freckles on her face,
Rosy cheeks, always happy,
Never living in disgrace.

Blonde hair, blue eyes,
Always smiling, never sad,
Rosy cheeks, always happy,
Never naughty, never bad.

Me and my best friend,
Always play with each other,
We invite our best friend round our house,
We even know each other's mother.

Josie Burgess & Tamryn Horner (10)
Cage Green Primary School, Tonbridge

Teacher

T is for teachers drinking tea in the staffroom
E is for Ed my teacher, he's really fun and cool
A is for Mr Liddle eating apples at break
C is for crumbs that the teachers leave behind
H is for the horrible teachers
E is for eventually we are allowed to go home
R is for rudeness around the staffroom.

Emma Cutts (8)
Cage Green Primary School, Tonbridge

Lauren Burton

L ollies are so sweet
A nd taste like strawberry
U nwrap a tasty lolly
R ed lollies are great to eat
E at all the lollies, but they are unhealthy
N ever put lollies on the floor

B ullseye's are very big and yummy
U sually they get sticky
R ound and juicy
T wo sweets got eaten
O h I want to have one
N early I'm going to have two.

Lauren Burton Bristow (7)
Cage Green Primary School, Tonbridge

Playground

P is for people chatting very loud
L is for laughing like the telly in your lounge
A is for children running around and around and around
Y is for yoghurt split on the ground
G is for girls screaming too loud
R is for ready, steady, go shouted by Mo
O is for oranges passed over to you
U is for umbrellas up, up and away
N is nuts scattered on the ground ready for children for play
D is for people having a happy day!

Poppy Powell (7)
Cage Green Primary School, Tonbridge

Mrs Bailey

Mrs Bailey is kind,
She has always got stuff on her mind,
Mrs Bailey is fun
And she loves everyone,
Mrs Bailey is groovy
And she always watches movies,
Mrs Bailey is fabulous with everyone in her class
And she gives out chewy bars,
Mrs Bailey is cool
And she is not a fool,
Mrs Bailey is great
And she is not overweight,
Mrs Bailey is wonderful,
She is always joyful,
Mrs Bailey is a great teacher
So you better be in her class.

Sarah Ford (10)
Cage Green Primary School, Tonbridge

Good Playtime

One lovely, sunny day,
We went out to play,
I always watch football
People play.

I hate it when we have to go in,
You have to do boring work,
I like my teacher today,
He is better than yesterday's.

When I go out after lunch,
I am so happy,
That I got out to play!

Natalie Rousell (8)
Cage Green Primary School, Tonbridge

Our World

Flowers purple
Apples green
Peaches orange
Cobras mean.

Elephants large
Insects small
Hippos short
Giraffes tall.

Hyenas laugh
Budgies talk
Dogs howl
Parrots squawk.

Reds stop
Greens go
Cheetahs fast
Snails slow.

Andrew Seaman (9)
Cage Green Primary School, Tonbridge

Playtimes

P laytimes are cool
L ater on at school
A fter we go in
Y esterday was a din
T oday is okay
I t always is
M r Liddle is thinking
E mma is drinking
S chooldays are boring.

Samantha Burton (8)
Cage Green Primary School, Tonbridge

Disgusting School Dinners!

School dinners, school dinners,
It makes me so sick!
Worms in spaghetti
And custard that's thick.

Dinner lady tells me off
If I leave one pea.
She's very, very bossy,
You wouldn't like to be me!

Kayleigh Phillips (8)
Cage Green Primary School, Tonbridge

Stinky Food

M is for mealtime with stinky food
E is for eggs with gone off middles
A is for apples with a very tasty crunch
L is for liver with a lovely, rubbery taste
T is for tasty, tangy tomatoes
I is for ill, poorly pupils
M is for mushy peas in potatoes
E is for eggy smells of eggs.

Alice Burgess (8)
Cage Green Primary School, Tonbridge

Toilets

T oilets smelling very bad
O h someone clean it out
I t smells of polluted air
L et it get cleaned, I will sir
E veryone can come in, it smells brilliant
T aps are OK, polluted air has gone
S oap is nice, but will it go?

Daniel Lincoln (8)
Cage Green Primary School, Tonbridge

Danny Brown

D azzling Danny
A mazing boy
N ever bad
N ever eats his greens
Y apping on all the time

B ouncing around
R unning round the house
O ver the beds
W aving
N ever eats fruit.

Danny Brown (8)
Cage Green Primary School, Tonbridge

Monkey

M arvin the magic monkey
O ver the top
N aughty monkey
K idnapped you
E ffective monkey
Y anking the net

M agic
A nice monkey
N icked you.

Cameron Hickmott (7)
Cage Green Primary School, Tonbridge

Fish

Fish can swim really well,
They live under the water,
They are all different colours,
Red, green and blue,
They play hide-and-seek.

Joe Gower (8)
Cage Green Primary School, Tonbridge

Teachers

Mrs Bailey is no fun
Mr Bishop plays the drum
Mr Anscomb is a price
Miss Holmes is very nice
Mrs Roberts has a brace
Mrs Turk is full of grace
Mrs Grant doesn't pay
Mr Liddle's birthday is in May
If you think they are bad
Mrs Miller can be sad.

Ashley Seamer & Liam Brown (10)
Cage Green Primary School, Tonbridge

Teachers

Mrs Science wears a wig
Mr Maths eats like a pig
Mrs English never watches telly
Mr Cook can't make jelly
Mrs Biology is a cry baby
Mr PE runs like a lady
But if you think they are stupid
Mrs Boss thinks she's cupid.

Thomas O'Toole (10)
Cage Green Primary School, Tonbridge

Sweets

S weet and sour
W onderful and wondrous
E njoyable and delicious
E normous and excellent
T asty treats
S uper sugary sweets.

Cyan Morris (10)
Cage Green Primary School, Tonbridge

Goal!

F ootballs are good, but not always
O ff people go if they're not good
O fficers are needed because people are bad
T ackle the players and take them out
B all go up and down
A ll players are skilful
L ay goals off and watch them go in
L ie to the refs and you will get sent off.

Jack Owen (11)
Cage Green Primary School, Tonbridge

Fruity Teachers

Mrs Apple is no fun
Mr Narner smacked our bum
Mr Carrot is so hairy
Mr Turnip is so scary
Mrs Plumb won't brush her hair
Miss Peach took our bear
But if you think they are mad
Mrs Kiwi's school isn't sad.

Adam Thomas Madgett (10)
Cage Green Primary School, Tonbridge

My Granny, Annie

My granny, Annie, yes I love her so,
From when I was little she could never let me go,
I care a lot about her, like she does for me
And when I'm with her, I'm happy and I always will be,
I pray for her and hope that she will never die
And if she does, I know that she'll be watching me from the sky.

Lauren O'Toole (10)
Cage Green Primary School, Tonbridge

Sea World

I went to Sea World and saw a demon shark
And a dolphin with a birthmark.
A black and white killer whale,
With a fish attached to its tail.
I caught a star which could wish,
His name was Fish,
I went for a swim and saw a water turtle called Moaning Murtle,
I saw sea horse on a funny racecourse,
I saw a puffer fish dancing with a rockfish,
I went for another swim, guess what I saw?
I saw an eel, his name was Bill,
I met a blue whale making sandcastles with a pail,
I saw a jellyfish, he chased me round a dessert dish,
I came across a shoal of tuna,
When above my head sailed a schooner.
I saw a duck-billed platypus, making such a fuss.

Cheryl Gray (10)
Cage Green Primary School, Tonbridge

Chocolates

C reamy insides of chocolate bar
H azelnut whirls melting in your mouth
O riginal chocolate recipe
C adbury's hollow cream egg
O range flavoured Terry's chocolate
L ovely, luscious chocolate
A musing sugary chocolates
T wisted, twirly chocolate
E dible Milky Way
S weets for a special, occasional treat.

Ellisha Owen (10)
Cage Green Primary School, Tonbridge

Maggie And The Dinosaur

At last they were out in the open,
Out in the shining sun,
Maggie started to look around,
And saw a delicious bun!

They headed for McDonald's
And fed the ducks on the way,
They realised they had no money
And knew they had to pay.

Off they went to the park,
Maggie saw the swings,
Dino got over excited
And wished he had fluttery wings!

They left the park and headed home
And carefully crossed the road,
They were just about to open the door . . .
When they trod on a slimy toad.

Kieran Obbard (10)
Cage Green Primary School, Tonbridge

Teachers, Teachers

Mr Tiddles
Shops at Lidel's
Miss Moles
Is scared of holes,
Mr Backchat
Plays with cats,
Miss Pear
Does really care,
But if you think they are silly
Mr Plum is so dumb.

Katie-Ann Blake (10)
Cage Green Primary School, Tonbridge

Sleepover Nights

S aying things about boys
L ovely hairstyles
E ating chocolates all night
E veryone goes crazy
P laying 'Dare' games
O n the floor is make-up
V ery loud girls
E verybody gets sleepier
R oom's very noisy

N obody else allowed
I n bed at midnight
G reat fun for hours
H aving a great time
T elling each other secrets
S sshh! The girls are going to sleep!

Emma Hopton (11)
Cage Green Primary School, Tonbridge

Liverpool Crazy

Liverpool are really cool,
But what they are to me,
I cannot name all,
Ball in net,
They'll regret,
They are first rate
And others do hate,
Premiership took 'em down,
They really do deserve,
A massive crown . . .

Phillip Rooke (11)
Cage Green Primary School, Tonbridge

Football

Football's great, but then it's bad,
When I went to the football match,
I did a great catch.
The audience thought it was wrong to do that,
So I asked my best friend Matt.
He said that was fine,
So I played on and threw it through a kite.
I was disqualified,
For ripping a hole in a poor little kite.
I bought him another one,
But the number of goals I scored was none!
I was so sad,
To know I was mad.
I gave up football and ran off to Liverpool.
Football's great, but it will soon be
Public enemy number one!

Carl Reeves (10)
Cage Green Primary School, Tonbridge

Brothers

B is for breaking everything in sight
R is for being rough every day and every night
O is for outstanding aggravation
T is for throughout giving me frustration
H is for hate inside and out
E is for enthusiastic I want to give him a clout
R is for rough, he's never a delight
S is for sizing me up for a fight.

Luke Riddall (11)
Cage Green Primary School, Tonbridge

God

God is in the air on a pair of wings
Looking down on all kinds of things

He is looking at all of you and your teams
Football, netball, hockey, sporty things

God is with you through good times
Helping you get through bad times

He's flying low, flying high
Even flying through the sky.

Jonathan Rodgers (11)
Cage Green Primary School, Tonbridge

Arsenal Rock!

Arsenal always win,
Never lose a game,
They play fantastic,
What a great goal,
They have won,
The Premiership Cup,
The other day,
Hip! Hip!
Hooray!

Chloe Palmer (11)
Cage Green Primary School, Tonbridge

Numbers

N is for numbers, odd ones and evens
U is for units of measurements
M is for maths, subtracting and times
B is for boring numbers in addition
E is for equilateral triangle
R is for rounding-up numbers
S is for solving problems, hard and easy.

Alex Richardson (11)
Cage Green Primary School, Tonbridge

Hallowe'en

H is for all the horrible creatures
A is for aliens dripping saliva over you
L is for you in your house, all lonely
L is for flickering lights
O is for an orange pumpkin
W is for all the wicked witches
E is for all the earwigs
E is for an unusual evening
N is for the next day, back to normal!

Charlotte Winchester (11)
Cage Green Primary School, Tonbridge

Stars

Stars,
Exploding balls of flames in space,
Exploding, flaming, hot,
Like a giant light bulb,
Like 3000 ovens flaming up,
It makes me feel cheerful,
It makes me feel like I'm in a huge microwave,
Stars,
Makes me think of my family.

Neale Upton (10)
Canterbury Road Primary School, Sittingbourne

Magic

Magic, magic everywhere
Magic here, magic there.
Magic at night when you're in bed
If you think of it, it comes to you.
Magic can be seen only when you dream
Bye-bye magic, it has gone.
You see, magic only comes at night.

Lucy Warner (7)
Canterbury Road Primary School, Sittingbourne

My Auntie, Cath

My auntie Cath is crazy
She drives my nanny mad
When her car runs out of petrol
Daddy says she's bad.

Her hair keeps changing colour
What will it be today?
Last time it was bright blue
And I just thought, *no way!*

She once took us on holiday
To Great Yarmouth we did go
We nearly went to Wales that day
How? We do not know!

I love my auntie Cath.

Amy Bowling (7)
Canterbury Road Primary School, Sittingbourne

Hamsters

Hamsters are sleepy
Hamsters are fidget bums
Hamsters are funny
And hamsters are clever.

Hamsters are lovely
Hamsters are hungry
Hamsters are sweet
And hamsters are cute.

Hamsters are furry
Hamsters are fast
Hamsters are small
I love hamsters.

Sam Cinderey (7)
Canterbury Road Primary School, Sittingbourne

Having Fun

I love fun, it's good for all
Fat or thin, short or tall
Playing tennis or football
Run, jump and sometimes fall.

In all weathers it doesn't matter
Hear the kids all scream and chatter
Waving flags and singing songs
Come join in and play along.

Watching telly, playing in the park
Playing in the sunshine, playing in the dark
Playing on my own, playing with my brother
Playing with my dad, playing with my mother.

But best of all I like playing with my mates
Leaping over fences, jumping over gates
Puffing, panting, sweating, soaking wet
Zooming round the streets like an airforce jet.

When I've have enough and tired in my head
I wash my sweaty body, then I go to bed
Sleep to charge my batteries, energy to regain
I get up in the morning, then start it all again.

Luke Ansley (7)
Canterbury Road Primary School, Sittingbourne

Art

I like drawing, painting too,
Cutting shapes, sticking with glue.
Pastels, chalks, red, blue and white,
Charcoal sticks, black as night.
Lots of materials like paper and card,
Papier mâché, messy then hard.
Find your best picture and put it in a frame,
Drawing and painting, I like this game.

Ross Ansley (10)
Canterbury Road Primary School, Sittingbourne

Looking Out The Window

Looking out the window
Watching all the birds
Singing in the morning
As the bees
Take the honey out of the flowers
Butterflies flying
People passing
All these things I see
Looking out the window
Looking out the window
Watching all the bees
Buzzing all around
The flowers and the trees
All these things I see
Looking out the window.

Hannah Daisy Kaur (7)
Canterbury Road Primary School, Sittingbourne

My Dog

Glossy fur
Pleading eyes
Wagging tail
Bounding paws
Chomping teeth
Sniffing nose
Sun loving
Bubble eating
Toy destroyer
Teddy stealer
Ice cube cruncher
Water seeker
Face washer
Best friend.

Amber Fletcher (7)
Canterbury Road Primary School, Sittingbourne

The Ocean

Diving and splashing,
A mini world,
Like an army of fish swimming by.

Sharks and whales are the kings,
Carp are the lawyers, the important ones,
Whereas minnows are the workers.

Working together like one, big family,
Helping each other out,
Spread all over the world.

Their world is huge against ours,
Making us feel so small,
With so many deadly creatures.

The ocean is a great place,
Where we all want to be,
But only fish live there,
In the deep blue sea!

Natalie Petch (11)
Canterbury Road Primary School, Sittingbourne

Monsters

Monsters under the stairs,
Purple skin and slimy, green hairs.
Moaning and groaning,
Wanting to be free.
Slimy, sickly, smelly things,
Burping, making rude noises.
The sound of them,
Stays in my head.
They're even under my bed,
Everywhere.
The stairs are exploding,
Oh no! They're terrorising the whole world!

Charlie Rochester (11)
Canterbury Road Primary School, Sittingbourne

Monster

Mum, Mum, there's a monster under my bed!
No, there isn't, go to sleep.
But he might gobble me up with his dirty, yellow teeth,
Or wrap me up with a piece of meat
To make me taste nice and sweet.
He might drag me under the bed and eat me up
And he might snort like a hog.
Did I say his breath smells like a bog?
Mum, Mum, there *is* a monster under my bed!
Not anymore, I chopped off his head!

Nicole Mitchell (11)
Canterbury Road Primary School, Sittingbourne

The Bird

The bird in the tree
Looks funny to me
And as I glance
It seems to say
In its own little way
I have stayed here long enough today
Now just watch me fly away
Hope to see you another day!

Lauren Garwood (10)
Canterbury Road Primary School, Sittingbourne

School

The teachers are like crocodiles
Hunting for their food
The children are like chickens
Scared of their teachers
The teachers snap
So the children run all the way home.

Jade Read (11)
Canterbury Road Primary School, Sittingbourne

My Pet, Fred

My pet, Fred
Has been around for years
Small, cute, furry
Like a fire-breathing dragon
Like a cheetah running around
It makes me feel big
Like a giant they all notice
My pet, Fred
Reminds me, how sweet life can be.

Jade Blythe (10)
Canterbury Road Primary School, Sittingbourne

The Never-Ending Space

Full of planets and stars
Great, beautiful, magnificent
Like an endless hole
Like a marble filled with glitter
It makes me feel like I'm floating
Like a feather in the wind
The never-ending space
Reminds us of time and reality.

Guy Cornelius (10)
Canterbury Road Primary School, Sittingbourne

Monsters

M onsters, monsters under my bed
O range, green, yellow and blue
N ever, never, never nice
S illy, stupid, eating glue
T easing, tiny, doing the tango
E ating through the bedside table
R unning, running, getting closer . . . *munch!*

Charles Bowling (10)
Canterbury Road Primary School, Sittingbourne

Dragons

Dragons large and dragons tall
And dragons so magical
You can't see them at all
Fire, electric, water and rock too
With all these powers, they will crisp you
Grind your bones and make their bread
They will do much worse instead
Some smart, some dumb
Some babies who suck their thumb
Some strong, some weak
And some quite unique
They are the great beasts of the land
Jungle, forest, sea and sand.

Mark Sage (11)
Canterbury Road Primary School, Sittingbourne

Hawk

The hawk
Built for speed
Small, fast, black
Like the midnight sky
And the beak looks
Like a shooting star
It makes me feel so slow
Like a baby tortoise
Plodding along, looking lazy
The hawk
Reminds us of how fun it would be
If humans could fly.

Joshua Wise (10)
Canterbury Road Primary School, Sittingbourne

The Snow Queen

Dancing snowflakes, mighty cold,
Misty airs cover a secret passage.

A breath of a woodman
Makes the ice queen stronger,
Snowflakes make a white carpet
For the queen.

Whoever qeustions the queen
Will fall to their death.
Her call echoes
The frosty land.

A chill runs down your spine
When her presence is near,
And darkness falls
Near.

Haylie Cinderey (10)
Canterbury Road Primary School, Sittingbourne

Different Seasons

At the beginning of the year it is spring,
Lambs come, birds sing.
Next, it's summer, it's funner,
We all go down to the beach
And I get a colour on my cheeks.
Next, it's autumn, it's very important,
Golden fruit grows on the trees
And don't forget to eat your peas.
Next, it's winter, I didn't get one splinter.
They hurt me.
Now you have heard all year round,
Look at all the different seasons we have found.

Leah Bliss Creamer (8)
Canterbury Road Primary School, Sittingbourne

Spring

As the trees swayed in the gentle breeze,
Their leaves danced in the light of the sun,
Aiming to please.

As I sat in my garden enjoying the view,
I could hear through the arch
Where the jasmine grew
Whispering leaves as they blew.

As evening fell and the birds began to roost,
The whispering leaves began to *ssshh* . . .
With the smell of honeysuckle in the gentle breeze,
The leaves have done all they could to please.

After sitting a while,
I decided to go,
I'll come back tomorrow
For another spring show.

Alana McFarland (7)
Canterbury Road Primary School, Sittingbourne

Monsters!

Monsters are taking over the world,
'Help, help!' there are ones with horns
And you can't forget . . . they eat prawns,
The breath smells like goo,
It scares me when they say, 'Boo!'
'Help, help!' there are monsters everywhere.

Big ones, fat ones, skinny ones, ugly ones,
They live under beds and sleep in threads,
They sleep in tellies, in their wellies,
One that has bones! Who moans and groans,
There's one under my bed who *screams!*
'Gonna get ya! Gonna get ya!'

Danielle Deeprose (11)
Canterbury Road Primary School, Sittingbourne

The Tombstone

In the black, midnight sky,
It's pitch-black now,
So no birds fly.
I start to run,
Then I trip,
Fall on my bum.
I hurt my backbone,
But still got up
And then I saw a creepy tombstone.
Then I saw him,
Who?
Count Mut.
We had a fight,
I kicked his butt.
He's gone back now,
He's scared of me,
I smashed him back down
And don't know how.

Graham Mark Coleman (11)
Canterbury Road Primary School, Sittingbourne

Monsters

Monsters are scary
Some are even hairy
They might give you a fright
In the middle of the night.

They might sleep under your bed
And take your best ted
They are better than snakes
At giving you a headache.

Some are really tall
Some are really small
So watch out
Monsters are about!

Hannah Tweed (7)
Canterbury Road Primary School, Sittingbourne

Monsters!

Big, slimy,
Long and hairy,
Big and ugly,
Fat and scary.
Puss on fingers,
Baggy eyes,
Covered in nits,
Covered in flies.
Foamy mouth,
Sharp teeth,
Long hair,
Smelly feet.
Loud roar,
Long nails,
Fat lips,
Short tails.
Monsters come in all shapes and sizes,
They hide under your bed and in your houses.
What's that? It looks like a troll!
Oh no! It's a monster . . .
And it's swallowed me *whole!*

Sophie Lotinga (11)
Canterbury Road Primary School, Sittingbourne

Ice Cream Haiku

Dripping down the cone
As a red, long tongue comes out
And licks it clean, yum!

As the flake breaks, oh
I pick it up and eat it
It's so nice now.

It drips down my chin,
It's all cold now, nice and cold,
I slurp it up, yum!

Chloe Dale (10)
Canterbury Road Primary School, Sittingbourne

Roller Skates

These were my brand new, blue ones,
They were the latest model in town.
I'd got them for my birthday,
Time to test them out.
I pull them on,
Do up the laces,
Perfect!
I set off
Down the drive,
Wind in my hair,
Sun in my eyes,
Along the road,
Past the corner shop,
Over the kerb,
Across the road,
Then . . .
Aaarrgghh!
I'm lying on the path,
A crumpled heap,
Blood pours from my head.
I'm not going on them again,
My brand new roller skates.
I'll put them away
And try skateboarding instead!

Melissa Gibbs (10)
Canterbury Road Primary School, Sittingbourne

Bulldogs

Bulldogs, bulldogs
They're the best
My dogs wear a vest
Bob, John, they're all dogs
They will never be hogs.

Kirsty Knight (11)
Canterbury Road Primary School, Sittingbourne

Pebbles

Beige and buff
Smooth not rough
Round and flat
Some thin, some fat
And some in-between.
Clattering, clinking
Clattering, clinking
The bumps and lumps
Beneath my feet
They roll in from the sea
As slippery as can be.
Rolling, nudging
Pushing, shoving
Shining, gleaming and
Basking in the sun.

Samantha James (11)
Canterbury Road Primary School, Sittingbourne

Dogs

My cuddly dog is called Amber
It was in a toy shop I found her
She is very pretty and sweet
But does not have anything to eat
My real dog, Sooty, is a boy
He likes to play with his toy
He has long, black hair
And hides under my chair
He jumps up and down for his food
But he is really very good
Dogs are the best pet
That's why I want to be a vet.

Emily Rose Thomson (8)
Canterbury Road Primary School, Sittingbourne

My Best Mate

I had an argument with my best mate today
It hurt, it really hurt.

We argued for ages
It went on and on.

I cried when I got home
I felt bad when I got home.

My phone went off, it rang and rang
I answered it, it was her.

We sat and spoke
She was happy, really happy.

We made up the very next day
I'm happy now, I'm really happy.

Nicole Jones (11)
Canterbury Road Primary School, Sittingbourne

Monster In My Cupboard

There's a monster in my cupboard
He won't come out to play
He eats his way through all my shoes
'Cause he's hungry every day.

There's a monster in my cupboard
He roars out loud each day
He eats his way through all the walls
And makes the neighbours pray.

There's a monster in my cupboard
He's silly, black and blue
I can't find him in my cupboard
Be careful, he could be after you!

Daniel Kirkham (11)
Canterbury Road Primary School, Sittingbourne

A Colour's Day

Aqua is dreaming at midnight,
Cloudy grey slowly opens his eyes.
Hazel munches on her breakfast,
Pale blue slowly pulls his clothes on.
Sunshine yellow skips her way to school,
Azure starts literacy at his desk.
Baby pink runs around at playtime,
Bright red starts her maths work at ten.
Navy-blue nibbles on a piece of toast,
Yellowy-green sits down to geography.
Magnolia sings the high notes,
Soft grey goes home to his family.
Creamy-white slowly trudges home,
Scarlet sits down all by herself.
Light green's head touches the pillow,
She is finally asleep tonight.

Stacey Louise Brooker (11)
Churchfields Primary School, Beckenham

Desert Island

The palm trees reach up to the hot, blazing sun,
The vast cliff tops stand there all day and night
Staring at the wild, rough, tossing sea,
Wild pigs hide in the long, swaying grass,
The swamp lays there, staring at the sun by day
And the stars by night,
The volcano spits liquid
Trying to knock the stars and sun out of the sky,
The hot, blazing sun peeps through the clouds,
As a sharp, jagged, fork of lightning
Tears up the earth.

Andrew Gerrans (11)
Churchfields Primary School, Beckenham

Colourful Shimmers

Waking up, by myself,
To the pale blue sky.

Getting dressed silently,
Like a fluorescent orange gleaming.

Brushing my teeth in time,
The pale pink seems to dance.

Eating breakfast to the beat,
Pale blue shimmers across my face.

Skipping down to see Bugs,
Rays of baby blue glisten.

Literacy acts like a shark,
Surrounding the pupils nervously.

Playtime with my friends,
Blood-red shines through my eyes.

Maths is tense,
When I can see nothing but indigo.

Lunch, play is waiting,
Metallic silver is the shimmer.

Rhoni Louise Allen (11)
Churchfields Primary School, Beckenham

Six Things Found In A Witch's Handbag

Green, slimy spot cream in a glass bottle
A dark, black hat covered with cobwebs
Dull, black, stinky, old, dusty lipstick
A black, greasy wig
Water in a rusty, old water pistol and . . .
A rotten piece of a broken broomstick.

Joe Williamson-Hicks (11)
Churchfields Primary School, Beckenham

Five Things Found In A Green Elf's Sack

A special net for catching golden magic dust,
Extra clean, green elf ears,
The complete spell book for green elves,
(Five grouts and 50 pickles at his local elf bookshop),
Jade green leaves, flowers and herbs to cure curses,
His magic, green, pointy hat (used when conjuring spells).

Rosie Stocking (10)
Churchfields Primary School, Beckenham

What An Irish Leprechaun Keeps In His Backpack

You know that an Irish leprechaun's backpack
Is filled with strange things
Like a four-leaf clover that brings you luck
Every time you look at it,
A magic bag for the tropical, patterned rainbow
To be stuffed in
And his green hat in the Irish-flagged backpack
That the little leprechaun carries on his back.

Sarah Rose Kenny (11)
Churchfields Primary School, Beckenham

My Saturday

Pale azure wakes up to breathe the fresh air,
Rose-yellow gets dressed for brekkie,
Concrete-grey joyfully eats breakfast,
Ruby-red rides his stunt bike,
Bright orange plays on his best mate's Xbox,
Grey is having his dinner,
Light green is watching 'Matrix Reloaded'.

Martin Parry (11)
Churchfields Primary School, Beckenham

Things You Would Find In A Witch's Cauldron

A slimy, squidgy eye of newt,
Would fall into your palm,
As you reach down
Further into the cauldron.

The bumpy legs of an octopus,
Would slither past,
As you reach down
Further into the cauldron.

Spices of all sorts,
Would tickle your nose with their scent,
Staining your hands with their tropical colours,
As you reach down
Further into the cauldron.

Spirits of the dead would awaken,
Grabbing your hand with their ice-cold fingers,
Pulling your arm down
Further into the cauldron.

Almost at the bottom now,
But as you touch the bottom of the pot,
A shrill cackle fills the air,
As you flee from the cave,
Flee from the witch
And definitely flee from the witch's cauldron.

Laura Walton (11)
Churchfields Primary School, Beckenham

What Is Your Day's Colours?

As the sun rises,
Pale blue wakes up
And is ready for the day,
Emerald green, slowly scrambles out of bed,
Deep azure blue gulps down its breakfast,
Shiny pale white quickly and quietly gets dressed,
A caterpillar, pale green, is playing with his football,
Orange has his lunch and sits down, calmly,
Indigo is calm and watches TV,
Pale violet is putting his PJs on,
Turquoise crawls into bed,
Now, pale blue drifts off to bed,
What is your day's colours?

Jack Featherstone (11)
Churchfields Primary School, Beckenham

Tropical Storm

As I entered the island,
A jewel was golden brown,
It felt soft on my feet,
As the storm brewed, I ran to shelter,
The lightning started to strike, like a cat to its prey,
The volcano erupted with an angry temper,
Rocks were being shattered by the sea's angry hands,
Trees being blown about, like feathers in a light breeze,
Coconuts falling, like bombs from a plane,
The island was calm no more,
Not like it was before.

Jackson Packer (10)
Churchfields Primary School, Beckenham

I'll Take Away With Me . . .

When I'm stranded on my desert island, I shall take . . .
The imagination of my friends to bring me cloudy dreams,
The love from my mum's heart to lead me on my way,
The ghost of my great nan to comfort me when I'm alone,
The sound of my cousin's accent all the way from New Zealand
And the feeling of my brothers holding hands.

Also I shall take . . .
The warmth of my friends for when I'm cold at night,
The happiness from my dad's laugh for when I'm tearful,
The soul of my great nan so I have a chance to come home,
The miaow of my cat to bring me love
And the feeling that I get when I'm tucked up in bed.

Rebecca Baker (11)
Churchfields Primary School, Beckenham

Secret Island

A climbing frame is a net waiting to attack
Dare to come near it will tangle you up
A flag is deadly it is a T-shirt caught in an updraft
Dare to come near it will
Slap! Slap! Slap!
Against you
Suddenly
The volcano spat
The wild waves crashed against the ragged rocks
Like wild pigs against the weak
The swamp
Dare to come near it will swallow you whole.

Samantha Offen (11)
Churchfields Primary School, Beckenham

A Desert Island

Lightning, lightning, near and far,
Leaving a scar near a star.

Palm trees, palm trees, standing around,
They are always glued to the ground.

Seashore, seashore, filled with fish,
There are even some jellyfish.

Sand, sand, on the seashore,
Sucking the sea through a straw.

Cliff, cliff, crumbling away,
Some of it will start to stray.

Volcano, volcano, lots of noise,
Which can start to annoy.

Elizabeth Irene Rae (11)
Churchfields Primary School, Beckenham

Desert Island

As the lightning strikes as powerful as a bomb,
The volcano is spitting lava.
As the sea's crackling as loud as thunder,
The rough coconuts fall.
As the stagnant swamp bubbles,
The bottles clatter together.
As the ships blow over the horizon,
The thunder roars.
As the pebbles roll off the cliff top,
The tide rolls in.

Lily Watkins (11)
Churchfields Primary School, Beckenham

It Roars

The volcano roars,
Like a bear hunting for food,
When the ship creaks,
The deck becomes un-nailed floorboards.
Lightning strikes,
Like a bullet out of a gun,
The reckless waves
Force the boats out to sea,
Wind catches the sails,
To pull the ship to shore,
Like a fan blowing through my hair.

Joshua Bysh (10)
Churchfields Primary School, Beckenham

Colour Cover

The beautiful colour of my eyes,
Show a nice yellow colour, like the sandy beach.
The nice green colour of the leaves,
Reminds me about the nice green apple.
When I'm watching TV,
The colour white shows up in front of my face.
Dark brown is the colour,
Of a nice, creamy chocolate.
Light blue reminds me of the sea.

Sean Michael Williams Carmody (10)
Churchfields Primary School, Beckenham

The Things In The Desert Island

The sun is a hot fireball,
It heats the people and they moan all day long.
The volcano is a huge rock, filled with lava,
It roars every so often, threatening to burst,
Causing trouble.
The sea is like a wild snake, hissing,
There are pebbles on the sand
That are bumpy and ragged,
They're ready to trip people over and laugh.

George Davis (11)
Churchfields Primary School, Beckenham

How Would You Feel If . . .

Lightning, lightning strikes the Earth,
With its jagged, bright light.

As fast as a cheetah,
As quick as a storm.

It claws the Earth,
As it shakes.

The sea goes wild,
While the waves go round.

Kele Onuoha (10)
Churchfields Primary School, Beckenham

Desert Island

On my desert island I would take . . .
Light blue glistening dreams,
A goodnight kiss from my mum and dad,
The cuddly feeling from my dog,
Giggles from my sister and brothers,
Playful things in my mind,
All the happiness from my family,
My best friend's voice,
All the dancing in my feet and arms,
Sunshine following me,
The wishes I wish to do.

Kayleigh Brotherwood (10)
Churchfields Primary School, Beckenham

The Storm

The platform of the tree house clangs in the wind,
The nets dance to the thunder.
Palm trees drop their coconuts onto the sand,
The volcano spits with a loud roar.
Storm clouds gather over like galloping horses,
Sand glistens whilst in a hurricane.
Everything turns wild
Then they . . .
Stop.

Hannah MacLennan (11)
Churchfields Primary School, Beckenham

Sporty Elf

When I was walking down the road,
I met a horrible elf,
I thought he was going to do some magic on me,
But he just wanted to help,
He asked me if there is anything wrong,
And I said, 'Yes.'
I told him all my troubles and problems
And then he said, 'OK.'
He took off his JD Sports bag and told me to say - check,
The elf sat down and started reading out:

'Have I got my ears? - Check
What about my wagon? - Check
How about my pears? - Check
And my cute pet dragon? - Check
Have I got my good dreams? - Check
And have I got my bad dreams? -Check
Have I got my poo ball? - Check
And my big, fat, cheese pool? - Check.'

He got back up and said to me,
'You do not need a remedy,
All you need is your friends back.'
And with that, he packed up his sack
And said, 'I'm going to JD Sports,
To get a new rucksack.'

Robia Brown (11)
Churchfields Primary School, Beckenham

The Commentator

What a wonderful match here today in Dave's back garden -
I mean Twickenham!
All the best have played before and these men (or boys) are
as quick as them
And let's start, it's Alex with the kick-off
Dave catches and runs
What skill, Aggh! What a tackle very rough
Passes to Matt, he's one that's tough
And Billy;
And Ben
He scored again! Amazing
And again, Alex with a kick-off
And oh no!
It's gone into Mr David's garden!
The ball is gone
Well, he's now done!
And all we can hear is . . . pardon
With Mr David's deafness
And all the time we'll never get it back
Alex will whine,
We'll search for another one
Under the furniture
Popular places
Until the frowns come up on our faces
But wait, he produces another
The frowns reduce, we're ready to play.

Jamie Russell (10)
Holy Family Primary School, Addlestone

Heaven Adventure

At ten fifteen, late at night,
A bang on the window gave me a fright.
Out of the window, I did stare,
And in the air I saw a flying mare.
Her mane was silky, fair and smooth,
Glistening and shiny, were her hooves.
And then, a pair of wonderful things,
Were this horse's astonishing wings.
I jumped up suddenly, scared like a stork,
When I found out this creature could talk.
She said, 'Come on! Climb on my back.'
In her voice, elegance did not lack.
We flew over the town, with the stars,
It seemed we were flying up to Mars.
With all of this I fell asleep,
But I woke up with a weep.
My horse trotted back tall and proud,
She said, 'You see we're on the clouds.
Alice, you see we're not in Devon,
Look around us we're in Heaven.'
I was so excited it was like a candyfloss ball,
Then I saw Great Aunt Georgina and Grandpa Paul.
On a cloud cross-legged we sat,
We shared gossip, we had a chat.
Then came the best bit of all,
I got to meet Angel Gabriel.
He also had wings, a halo too,
In Heaven people there were many, angels a few.
Then came the time I had to go,
I said 'Goodbye', but I wanted to say 'Hello.'

Alice Smith (10)
Holy Family Primary School, Addlestone

Life

I look out on the garden
From inside and from out
And if you give me pardon
This is what it's about.
We fight our way right through it,
Through trouble and through strife
And every day we do it
We do what I call life.

In death we are an honour
Or so say the Klingons
But it's life that has more of 'er
Maybe it's not as long,
Maybe death is eternal
By the stab of a knife,
But if you read the journal
First place would go to life.

In life we have potential
To have peace and have fun
And when someone goes mental
In death we cannot run
Then comes the resurrection,
It has beauty and great sight.
We're back with full perfection
Reintroduced to life.

Then we sit and remember
What we did wrong and right
And realise nothing's tender
As a full adventurous life.

Rowan Brearley (10)
Homefield Preparatory School, Sutton

If You're Thinking About Getting A Cat

If you're thinking about getting a cat
You need to get a basket
Did you know that?
It needs to be comfy, snug and warm
In a room with no windows or places to explore.

If you're thinking about getting a cat
You need some cat food
Did you know that?
It needs to be placed in the same spot every day
So don't move it or it will never get nibbled away.

If you're thinking about getting a cat
You need a brush to groom it
Did you know that?
You need to groom it twice a day
Or else all those nasty fleas will never go away.

Jordan Brown (9)
Homefield Preparatory School, Sutton

Once Upon A Rhyme . . .

I want people to play with me
I want them to love and care for me
Then I would like them
And they wouldn't be scared of me

If people could groom me
I would like them to
If they could give me a basket
It would be a nice thing to do

I like fish it's my favourite food
But I need a dish to eat it in
And I need a bowl definitely
It has to be a special one or it will spill.

Haroon Taylor (9)
Homefield Preparatory School, Sutton

London

In England
Where I live
There are lots of sightseeing views
The biggest city of all is London
I go once a year

Lots of tourists come
From Japan, Korea and Milan
To the London Eye
I've been there
And the British Museum too

It takes an hour to get there
But I don't mind
I go by train
Then on the underground
In our great country.

Louis Pickard (9)
Homefield Preparatory School, Sutton

Favourites

L ook! There's Buckingham Palace
O h look, the marvellous BT Tower
N ext stop, Oxford Street
D o we have to eat in Marks and Spencer?
O h yes, we're going to Hamleys
N o! I don't want to go home.

O xford College here we come
X mas is the time of year
F or that is why we came to Grandpa's house
O h dear, the windscreen's frozen over
R eally, the city is beautiful
D o go and watch the boat race.

Maximillian Gorynski (10)
Homefield Preparatory School, Sutton

On Hearing 'Pavane Pour Une Infante Defunte'

The sound of trudging feet
A tiny coffin
Men weighed down by sadness
Enter church in a solemn march.

The organ soaring like a lark
As the choir gracefully assembles
Silhouetted by candles burning
People crying, sobbing.

A girl remembered
Nostalgia for the happy times
Sadness and crying inside
Outside putting on a brave face.

The congregation walks out
To join the family for last prayers
Raindrops and tears mix as the coffin is lowered
The men bowing as the final blessing is given.

Enough is enough
It has to stop
Ravel did not write his music
For unborn Iraqi children.

Ryan Drucker (11)
Homefield Preparatory School, Sutton

Action At The Wicket

C racking the bat
R uns at the wicket
I t's not that far
C atch it
K eeper shouts
E xcellent effort
T op spin gets a wicket.

Joshan Chana (9)
Homefield Preparatory School, Sutton

Gena The Lion

Gena, a lion at the zoo
Escaped without knowing what to do
He caused a lot of consternation
During rush hour at the station
He had an awful lot of fun
Chasing people on platform one
Thereafter running to the jewellery shop
He picked up diamonds he saw people drop
And thought of his keeper, Mr Ray
What he'd do when Gena got away
Suddenly an idea came to Gena's head
Why should I care while I'm ahead?
He rushed off to a billionaire's house
And quickly hunted down his spouse
The billionaire had everything under wraps
Hurrying off to turn on the taps
'I'll let her go,' he said of Gena afloat
'Who cares if the house has a moat?'
Gena thought it safer at the zoo
And asked what he should do
He hoped it wasn't too late
To be taken back to his mate
So in the end there was no more strife
As Gena and Mr Ray had a really great life.

Murtaza Hussain (11)
Homefield Preparatory School, Sutton

After Five Days

C ricket's wicked
R ough and tough
I n the square
C almly
K illing the ball
E nding the match
T he 'Test' is over.

Harry Ledger (10)
Homefield Preparatory School, Sutton

Confession

I blamed it on a lunatic,
I blamed it on my brother,
But I know that in the end I can't
Escape the wrath of my mother.

Shall I tell you now,
This sad tale of woe?
For it would trouble me a lot,
To see you (the reader) go.

Please don't spill this secret,
That I'm about to share.
Besides it wasn't my fault,
The house blew up, so there!

'Twas on a Sunday afternoon,
I couldn't resist the temptation.
All because Mum had refused,
To buy me some at the station.

In my search I overturned,
Anything that stood in my way.
How was I supposed to know,
That the cupboard could be toppled astray?

I reached up, standing on a stool,
Alas my hands were too short.
So I got up onto the table and then I felt
My foot in a collision caught.

Disaster struck, chaos ensued,
When I tripped over that jug.
I stumbled and rumbled and very, very soon,
The cupboard met my impending mug.

Shelves dropped like dominoes, collapsing onto one another,
Then the boiler got into the way.
So I readied myself for the explosion,
By hiding under a large metal tray.

OK, maybe it was my fault,
But the government should get the blame really.
I mean, do we seriously need all that security,
To protect us from a terrorist who's a bit dreary?

Look, I'll just cut straight to the point,
I swear I'll never lie again.
I mean, my bodyguard Andy Gotlairy,
Doesn't even have the brains of a hen.

I've been keeping this lie up for so long,
I'm just sick and tired of this charade.
All I ever wanted,
Was just a glass of lemonade!

Timothy Hu (11)
Homefield Preparatory School, Sutton

The World Of Relaxation

If you want some fun
My garden's the place,
As the barbecue fries
And the hammock sways
In turn with the swings
You just sit and gaze.
Summer comes,
The flowers bloom
Lawns grow lush
And green quite soon.
The hose will leak
When the garden's watered,
The shed door creaks
As the wind blows,
The guinea pig squeaks,
The rabbit's feet thump,
The socks on the line fall
And you can hear my mum call.
A garden is full of adventure
I bet you want to come.

Richard Mortimer (10)
Homefield Preparatory School, Sutton

Your Frogginess

'I am the fairest frog of all,'
Exclaimed a handsome frog named Saul.
However, I can't say so much,
For the ugly frog named Hutch.

Hutch was ugly, thin and weak,
The expression on his face was bleak.
But, one thing no one recognised,
Was the handsome prince inside.

You see, Hutch had a spell upon him,
By the wicked witch,Ilongym.
She was jealous of his gorgeous looks
And the way he read fairy tale books.

The one true way to break the spell,
Required a person to really yell.
But this person could not be ordinary,
Just the leary lad from the local dairy.

I know you're thinking that shouldn't be hard,
But the dairy folk would not leave their yard.
Poor old Hutch would have to go to them,
An act that the witches would condemn.

So leary Isaac from the dairy,
Conjured up a magic fairy,
At once the spell backfired with a boom,
'Ha! Ha!' laughed Hutch, 'the witch will meet her doom.'

James Peattie (11)
Homefield Preparatory School, Sutton

Next Man In

C ricket is fun
R un, run, run
I t will come
C an you wait?
K itted out
E ating sandwiches
T rying to keep the nerves away.

Robbie Macdonald (9)
Homefield Preparatory School, Sutton

The Best

E lectrically powered
N ew cinemas and goods
G lorious at sport
L oving to the Queen
A nd best at rugby
N ever easily beaten
D irectly the best country on Earth.

Harjas S Shinmar (10)
Homefield Preparatory School, Sutton

Being Competitive

C ricket's action
R acing for a run
I saw a gap
C alling quickly, 'Yes!'
K eeper's end they shout
E at him up
T each him a lesson.

Patrick Souberbielle (9)
Homefield Preparatory School, Sutton

A Steam Train

Puffing, hissing
Gaining speed
Racing through countryside
Forming a line of smoke

The tunnel up ahead,
All quiet and sleepy
Then, *bang, crash, smash*
The train rockets through.

Green like a dragon
As loud as one too,
Puffing out smoke
From deep inside

It ruins the silence
It pollutes the air
That is the nature
Of the disappearing steam train.

Guy Aldous (11)
Homefield Preparatory School, Sutton

Where Is It?

Can you feel it in the air?
Can you see it in the Tate?
Can you smell it in Chelsea?
Can you taste it in the bars?
Does it have a good history?
Does it have good technology?
Does it have good sport?
Does it have nice people?
Is it strong in will?
Is it rich in spirit?
Is it a great place to be?
I'm glad I live in England.

Luke Sumner (10)
Homefield Preparatory School, Sutton

Freddie

Here is a poem about my hamster,
He'd tell you himself but he's not quite ready.
We named him after a football star,
We've even built him a Lego car!

He likes a grape or a bit of cheese,
Or even a bit of boiled egg please!
Into his pouches he stuffs it all,
Even the grape which looks like a ball.

At half-past six he runs about,
He squeaks in the air saying, 'Let me out!'
While I have a bath I let him free,
To stretch his legs and have a wee!

His life ambition before he should die,
Is to eat my very best Homefield tie.
Chewing the carpet is really quite bad,
It drives my mum completely mad!

The life of a hamster is really quite short,
Two years from the very first day he was bought.
I know I must soon say goodbye,
So he may join the hamsters in the sky.

Bradley Pfeifer (11)
Homefield Preparatory School, Sutton

The Raccoon

Silently scavenging through the bin
Hoping to find food, anything will do.
Distinctive eyes like glowing lights
Shine through a bandit's black mask.
Bushy tail as soft as snow
With rings bold as lightning.
And in the spring the thick fur moults
Its winter coat vanishing.

Daniel Aldham (11)
Homefield Preparatory School, Sutton

The Race

We line up in the starting block,
Oh no! Larry is injured; he will have to hop,
The starting gun has been fired,
Dave's off like a shot, but will soon be tired.

I think I'm doing well! I'm faster than my cousin,
However, my heart is beating fifty to the dozen.
Oh, I'm so glad, I'm more than two-thirds there!
What I would do for a lovely, juicy pear!

Last hundred yards, no longer a pain
I've cast aside the ball and chain!
I'm going well; I'm right in front of the string,
I've won! I've won! I am the king.

Nicholas Cleeve (11)
Homefield Preparatory School, Sutton

Felix The Cat

The sweetest of kittens
With four white mittens
Lives in our house on Wimbledon Hill

He eats all night
And sleeps all day
But in-between he likes to play

His favourite food is prawn
And mouse
He even brought one in the house

Lots of cuddles every day
He's even got
His hideaway.

Sam Chamberlain (11)
Homefield Preparatory School, Sutton

Principal Baddy

He's mean and hairy
Big and scary
His teeth go chomp
His feet go flomp

He eats children
Bones and all
I think that's why
He's grown so tall

His fingers are rocks
With an iron grip
No matter how hard I try
I can't give him the slip

Who is this menace?
Big and bad
The headmaster?
No - it's my dad!

James Forbes (11)
Homefield Preparatory School, Sutton

The Beach

Small waves roll up the beach
'Look out Mum, you'll get wet feet!'
Damp rocks strewn with seaweed
Glistening in the midday sun
The tide slowly rising
Then falling
Taking with it sand and seaweed
Spiky shells sticking out of soft, hot sand
The burning sun high in the sky
Marking the time of day.

George Cunliffe (11)
Homefield Preparatory School, Sutton

The Bully Bunch

The big bully bunch
Sat in a hunch
Looking for someone to smash

I pulled up my socks
Ready for the knocks
Content to give it a mighty big bash

He fell on the floor
Covered in gore
Making a loud and terrifying crash

They all ran away
I'd won the day
As they disappeared as fast as a flash.

Christopher Everest (10)
Homefield Preparatory School, Sutton

The Viking

There was a Viking
Who was the scariest in history
His name was Battleaxe
Which added to his mystery

No one disagreed with him
When he set sail on the *Wren*
If they did they'd be put on the rack
And never breathe again

Then a boat appeared out of the mist
That fired a cannonball
It struck at the Vikings
And caused them all to fall.

Timothy Eales (11)
Homefield Preparatory School, Sutton

The Ninja

Slowly walking
Silently stalking
A killer nears its prey
No chance to slip away

Dangerously infiltrate
Controlling its fate
Bracing for the kill
A Ninja waits its fill

Flash
   Slash
      Cries
         Dies

The Ninja moves away
Completes its unwelcome stay
No one will stand and fight
As it moves stealthily through the night.

William Gonsalves (11)
Homefield Preparatory School, Sutton

Lunch

It was waiting on a branch
Its prey coming closer
Unaware of any danger.
It was getting ready to pounce
As a tiny grey mouse appeared
Whoosh!
The mouse wiggled in a beak
Strong wing beats carrying it away
Then with a mighty gulp
The kestrel wasn't hungry anymore.

Felix Greenhalgh (11)
Homefield Preparatory School, Sutton

The Wind

The pine tree shook as it passed
Waking up birds in a nest
Flying down alleyways very fast
Never stopping, no need for rest

Whistling as it raced across a street
Crashing into a cold, brick wall
Blowing people off their feet
Watching small boys trying not to fall

Ripping roof tiles off the houses
Causing havoc in the town
Blowing madly up girls' blouses
Laughing at people as they frown

Suddenly behind a cloud
A beam of light lands on the ground
Somebody cheers aloud
The sun has settled without a sound.

Jaspal Chana (11)
Homefield Preparatory School, Sutton

Homefield Sevens

It was the Homefield Sevens
Several sides to fear
I looked up to the heavens
And did not hear
But felt them like thunder
The ball bouncing on our side
They were about to plunder
As it rolled to me, I couldn't hide
Off came the scrum cap, my disguise
There was the ball to catch
And take the lead, to my surprise
Time for an impact on the match
The chance to see the trophy and me
Success we hadn't seen since ninety-three.

Jamie Falconer (11)
Homefield Preparatory School, Sutton

Ban Homework!

I think homework is unfair,
It's not as if I don't care.
I work so hard all day long,
Surely a few hours off would not be wrong?

I'm sure I'm not the only one
Who, at the end of the day,
Just wants to have fun.
Maybe the teachers have nothing to do
But mark our work all night through?

I'm sure the teachers will agree
How much happier life would be
If we could *all* do our best at school,
And then at home, we could play it cool!

Simon Rodin (11)
Homefield Preparatory School, Sutton

Summer Holidays

Everybody's noisy, constantly chattering
Restlessly waiting for the bell to ring
Boys start racing through the door
Parents hear an excited roar
Watch them pouring across the tar
Teachers react to a screeching car
The school is suddenly as quiet as a mouse
The noisiest relaxing at his house.
A holiday spent lying in bed
Totally bored out of his head
He looks at the calendar every day
Can't wait for school to have his say
The magic first day always a sensation
After that he can't wait for the vacation.

Harry Gunn (11)
Homefield Preparatory School, Sutton

The Lonely Tree

Standing alone in the blazing sun
Except for the droning hum of summer bees
A young boy passing, eating a bun
And in the distance, a forest of trees
People scratch names into my bark
In this spot where for years I've stood
How lovely to be with others in the park
I would pick up my roots and walk if I could

A man approaches carrying spade and hoe
Not far from me, he digs some holes
Comes back later and puts in poles
Returns again with saplings to plant in a row
No longer just me, standing alone
But part of a crowd when my friends have grown.

James Stockwell (11)
Homefield Preparatory School, Sutton

The Chocolate Cake

There was once a chocolate cake
It really was so fine
Sweet and soft and with a flake
It tasted especially divine
I would get up every morning
And stumble down the stairs
I'd be at the fridge door yawning
Moving aside apples and pears
On the top shelf it is there
Appetising under sticky foil
With its creamy topping and chocolate fare
For me each day to enjoy the spoil
Who made it or why, I don't know
Best things just happen, it goes to show.

Jack Ledger (11)
Homefield Preparatory School, Sutton

Unwanted Heroes

Like unwanted daisies in winter fading
Slowly but surely
Great heroes no longer die in bloody feuds
They disappear, wrapped in old newspapers
By park benches
Where nobody cares.

Oliver Duffy (11)
Homefield Preparatory School, Sutton

The Way Of War

As they march down the road,
Guns upon their backs,
The plane gets loaded,
For the war is back.

Adults crying, children screaming
As their dads take off,
Over to Germany they fly
For the war is back.

Sirens are sounded,
Bombs are coming.
Fire and explosions are spread,
For the war is back.

Years have gone,
Children have left,
Houses have been bombed
For the war is back.

The war is over,
Not all have returned,
Children are scared to come back,
And that is the way of war.

Laura Gillham (11)
Hook Lane Primary School, Welling

Millwall

M is for Millwall the best team of all,
I is for Ifill who can definitely kick a ball,
L is for lions roaring at the den,
L is for loyalty from the boys and men,
W is for Wisey our manager and player
A is for always being top of the layer,
L is for laughing when we win the cup,
L is for lions, we are on the up.

Harry Pieske (11)
Hook Lane Primary School, Welling

Charlton

C harlton are the best, better than the rest
H ip, hip, hooray shouts the crowd
A t the break they have some tea
R ufus is the best at the rear
L isbe lies awake for the whole match
T ime for the whistle to blow, it has to go
O n the pitch they go
N obody can beat us we are the best, better than the rest.

Lewis Perkins (11)
Hook Lane Primary School, Welling

A Perfect Day

I see my horses
Eating green grass in the field
He gallops over to me
Like he hasn't seen me for days
I stroke his soft fur lightly
He rubs his head on my shoulder
Then the sun comes out brightly
I jump upon his back
And together we gallop off.

Grace Lacey (10)
Hook Lane Primary School, Welling

Leaving School

When I'm leaving school,
I'll bet I'll cry.
I'll miss my mates, my
Teachers too.

I'll bring a shirt,
For everyone to sign.
I'll bring my memories
With me.
Everywhere I go.

Alice Hunt (10)
Hook Lane Primary School, Welling

Shelly

Shelly is my rabbit,
She is brown and white.
Her fur is soft,
She sniffs the flowers that are bright.
Shelly is my rabbit,
She has floppy ears.
She loves eating carrots,
Foxes she fears.

Emma Budgen (11)
Hook Lane Primary School, Welling

Fireworks

The fireworks are ready to take off,
One after another,
They light,
And soar a hundred feet high,
All the colours and shapes in the sky make my eyes water,
The sounds soft, loud, all kinds of noises,
Bang, wallop, pop . . .
Gone.

Suzanna Wilkinson (11)
Hook Lane Primary School, Welling

Night-Time

I lie in bed,
I cannot sleep,
I look around,
And count some sheep.

I hear a noise,
What could it be?
I listen hard,
I cannot see.

I fall asleep,
And start dreaming,
There's a hippo,
That is beaming.

Emma Clarkson (11)
Hook Lane Primary School, Welling

Stage Fright

I'm on the stage,
Lights in my eyes,
I cannot see,
Surprise, surprise,
It's my turn now,
What do I say?
Oh no I can't remember!
Everyone's looking,
My forehead's cooking,
I open my mouth,
But no words come out!
I feel like I'm turning on a roundabout!
I need some help *now!*

Holly Baker (11)
Hook Lane Primary School, Welling

World War II

Please save us,
Blasting homes,
Killing people, WWII, blitzed Britain!

Please save us,
Evacuated children,
Lonely mothers, WWII, blitzed Britain!

Please save them,
Keeping animals,
Eat them too,
WWII, blitzed Britain!

Please save them,
Rubbled houses,
Destroyed lives,
WWII, blitzed Britain!

World War II, please no more wars!
Give peace and save the world!

Emily Kirk (11)
Hook Lane Primary School, Welling

My Baby Sister

My baby sister is such a nuisance
All she does is cry.
I can never get to sleep at night
Because she is a pain.
I wish, I wish she would go away
And never come back again.

She gets all the attention
Oh it is not fair.
They think she is an angel
And it doesn't seem fair.

Ellie Ganney (11)
Hook Lane Primary School, Welling

Autumn Leaves

Autumn leaves are falling,
In the cold midday sunshine,
The cool breeze is calling,
At the end of the day,
The autumn colours whirling,
Orange, yellow and green,
The crispy leaves are curling,
While lying on the dew.
The leaves crunch between my feet,
While others fall from the trees,
I love the autumn days,
Sounds, feelings, colours, fire,
Just my type of day.

Rachel Jones (11)
Hook Lane Primary School, Welling

I Wish

I wish I was a mermaid,
I wish I lived under the sea.
I wish I could be anybody,
As long as it wasn't me.

I wish I was on holiday,
I wish it was my birthday.
I wish I had a bunny,
I'd play with it everyday.

I wish I had a teddy bear,
I wish I had very long hair.
I wish I could be anybody,
But I'm happy just being me.

Charlotte Flack (11)
Hook Lane Primary School, Welling

Sirens And The Blackout

'The sirens, the blackout,
Quick get home!
Quick into the Anderson shelter!
The sirens, the blackout.
Shooting, dying.
The sirens, the blackout,
German planes lost,
English planes lost,
The sirens, the blackout.
Misleading signs
Crashing planes,
The sirens, the blackout.
I hate the sound of the sirens,
Oh, please stop the war,
The sirens, the blackout.'

Sean Delaney (10)
Hook Lane Primary School, Welling

My Nanny's Dog

I loved my nanny's dog,
She played with the cat
She chased out the rats,
But she couldn't stay alive forever.

She had a terrible pain,
We didn't like seeing her like this.

We took her to the vet
'I'm sorry but we have to put her down'
Whispered the vet,
We were all very sad but in a way glad
Because at least she wasn't living in pain.

Jamie Hutchinson (11)
Hook Lane Primary School, Welling

As Funny As A Clown

Born in jelly
Not a big belly

Swimming in the deep blue sea
Wiggling tails giggling with glee

Lives in anemone
With not a good memory

Orange and white
Lovin' the light

Great colliders
Minding the divers

Always hiding
As they're gliding

Sometimes funny whether big or small
These are clown fish after all!

Harry Smith (9)
Hook Lane Primary School, Welling

My Cats

I've got two cats
Annoying!
Scratching,
Biting,
Padding,
Leaving their hair
Everywhere!
But . . . they're my cats!

Michael Carr (10)
Hook Lane Primary School, Welling

Little Monsters

Little monsters under the bed
Little monsters dancing round in my head,
With their big hairy bodies
Coming to whip me away!

Little monsters under the bed
Little monsters dancing round in my head,
With their big slimy tongues
Coming to lick me when I sleep!

Little monsters made me cry
Mum came in and asked me 'Why?'
I told her, 'It's the monsters under my bed!'

Isabelle Flaherty (11)
Hook Lane Primary School, Welling

Glug-Glug

I am not a good swimmer,
I'm afraid of deep water.
At least I can swim,
And that is all that matters.

Swimming to the other side,
Puffing and panting.
I go back,
Sinking . . . splashing . . . crying.

Sinking down to the bottom,
Someone jumps in,
I got pulled out
Never again!

Sarah Powell (11)
Hook Lane Primary School, Welling

Blitz!

Crash! Boom! Blast!
I'm really scared!
I can hear bombs!
I'm in an Anderson shelter!
It's the *blitz!*

Crash! Boom! Blast!
My name is Sue
I'm ten tonight
I can't wait till it's over
I have a brother and a sister
We're in the *blitz!*

Crash! Boom! Blast!
It's nine o'clock
Now I'm ten
I got a *big* bar of chocolate
Now . . . I'm sick!
I hate the *blitz!*

Crash! Boom! Blast!
I'm still here!
I'm still fed up!
When will it end?
This is my story, of me in the . . .
Blitz!

Kim Stringman (11)
Hook Lane Primary School, Welling

My First Dancing Lesson

I tiptoed across the stage,
Dancing like a real ballerina.
Then I twirled,
Like a twister.
I also jumped,
So high I nearly touched the sky.

Zoe Ford (11)
Hook Lane Primary School, Welling

The Homeless Man

Help him by
Throwing him some money
When you walk past him in the street.
The homeless man.

Help him by
Keeping him company
On a cold, cold night.
The homeless man.

Help him by
Buying him a McDonald's
When you're getting one.
The homeless man.

Help him by
Taking him in for the night
When it's Christmas.
The homeless man.

Help him by
Buying him a coat
When it's cold.
The homeless man.

Help him by
Being his friend
When he hasn't got one.
The homeless man.

Tom Luff (10)
Hook Lane Primary School, Welling

Skipping (Cinquain)

Skipping
Skipping is fun
Jumping over the rope
We can limbo under the rope
So low.

Katie Simons & Emma Ray (9)
Hook Lane Primary School, Welling

Looking For A Friend

I'm looking for a best friend,
Someone just like me,
Someone good at football,
Someone smart and free . . .
I'm seeing someone special
Quite good-looking too.
Someone really clever,
Someone rich and true . . .
But hang on, you can be true
I know you, please will you be
My friend?

Chelsie Keeffe (9)
Hook Lane Primary School, Welling

Balloons

Blow the balloons up to the sky,
Look at them they're flying ever so high.

Look at the different colours blue, green and red,
Don't let go so you can take them to bed.

Let the balloons go, up, up and away,
Maybe you will see them another day!

Maddison Hoyle (8)
Hook Lane Primary School, Welling

Footie (Cinquain)

Footie
Is the greatest
The goals are fantastic
Henry is the best in the world
Footie!

Ashley Merredew (9)
Hook Lane Primary School, Welling

Football Crazy

Football crazy
Crazy about football
I really, really am
I support Arsenal
I'm a really good fan

They score a lot
With Theiry Henry
He's the main man
We could not do without him
So that's why I'm a fan.

George Bradford (9)
Hook Lane Primary School, Welling

Football Crazy

Football kicker,
Crazy scorer
Football skills,
Funny sliders
Cool players,
Mad field
Giant field,
Funny ball
Chequered ball.

Jamie Barnes (9)
Hook Lane Primary School, Welling

R I P

A man got hit on the shoulder,
With a very big boulder.
But now he's dead,
He's lost his head,
He won't get any older!

Thomas Barrett (9)
Hook Lane Primary School, Welling

Snow

It started off with thunder
Then it turned to lightning
Crash! Bang! Crash! Bang!

Snow is falling, look how strange
Let's go out to play

Snow angels, snowmen.
Look how beautiful Anna is,
Snowball fights,
Boys and girls playing all the time.

Hats, gloves, scarves, wellies and
Don't forget your coat.

Don't forget your snowman
This is what you need,
A carrot for the nose,
Some raisins for the eyes
Don't forget the hat and scarf
What a big surprise.

Megan Bardini (9)
Kingscroft Junior School, Staines

Snow

Snow here, snow there,
Snow everywhere,
Over the hills, over the fields,
Snowball fights and snowman making,
Skiing, sliding, skating
People falling over
Now it's getting warmer,
Ice is getting friskier,
People are getting sadder,
As the ice melts.

Paige Adams (9)
Kingscroft Junior School, Staines

Snowball Battle

Sliding in came the judge,
'Let the battle begin,'
Humans versus Snowball Zombies
They took a magic staff
The zombies started to laugh
The humans threw a blizzard
But it was not very round
It disappeared in a puff of smoke
Then stepped forward a little bloke
And started to build a snowman.

Its nose popped out and hit the zombie
It fell down without a sound
Then it got up again and stabbed him
Did the man with no tummy
If I did that I would get told off by my mummy
The next human stepped forward
Turned around, touched the ground
Then gave him a painful tango
The zombie died and that was the end of that.

Simon Green (10)
Kingscroft Junior School, Staines

Alone

Alone, the worst feeling you could have,
Like your soul has drifted away to a distant land.
And there's nothing you can do about it,
Like all the fish in the sea have swum away.
Maybe they'll come back another day.

Michael Brown (10)
Kingscroft Junior School, Staines

Snow

One night it snowed
While I was asleep,
When I got up,
I had a peep.

What I saw
Was snow everywhere,
I thought it was a dream
Because it couldn't be a nightmare.

As I walked to school,
I saw snowmen
Much, much smaller
Than tall Big Ben.

Jason Cheung (10)
Kingscroft Junior School, Staines

Snow

Snowmen we build,
All day long,
Snowflakes fall,
The ice is very strong.

We make a lot of snowballs,
And then throw them at our friends,
We make a lot of snowmen,
With the weather the sky sends.

We've had all the fun now,
It's time for the snow to go,
No more snowball fights,
Just normal, boring nights.

Kerry Hunter (10)
Kingscroft Junior School, Staines

Cows!

When I was walking in Dorset with glee
This poem reminded me.
The cows behind the river
And grass snakes slither.
'Moo, moo' the cows say,
What a lovely day.

Their beautiful reflection in the river
From the cows sharing with the
Snakes that slither.
Baby calves
And the flying doves.
The blue sky with wild clouds
As the sheepdogs howls
Cows, cows, cows.

Rosy Lord (9)
Kingscroft Junior School, Staines

Snow

Snowman, skating, falling snowflakes totally white
It felt so right.

It's so exciting,
That's what I'm writing.

With a hot cup of chocolate I sat by the window
But now the snow is falling very slow oh,

It's stopped now but it sill looks beautiful
It looks like my garden is covered with snow.

Carol-Anne Coop (10)
Kingscroft Junior School, Staines

Snow

One night I fell asleep
I couldn't resist a little peep;
I pulled up the blind and looked at the snow
My mum walked in and said, 'No, no!'
I went back to sleep
Dreaming about the snow
I woke up in the morning
And it was gone . . .
I shouted, *'Nooo!'*
I went outside to see down the road
To see if it really, really had snowed
Or maybe it was a dream all this time
But it couldn't have been
It looked so fine!

Abigail Musk (9)
Kingscroft Junior School, Staines

Go To Sleep

One night I fell asleep,
I had to have a little peep,
I pulled down the blind,
And what did I find,
Beautiful white snow,
And my dad said, 'Oh no!'

Dad said 'Go back to sleep,
You're not allowed another peek,
You have to go back to sleep!'
I thought it must be a dream,
It tastes like ice cream.

Dominic Galvin (9)
Kingscroft Junior School, Staines

Snow

Snow, snow
Wonderful snow
Watch it fall
Watch the heaps grow.
Freezing fun
Happy and icy weather
People going to performances
Such as Disney on Ice.
White snow icicles
Weird blizzards,
Wet, beautiful igloos
Snowmen, snowball fights, Eskimos.
But when the sun comes out,
Snowflakes are no more.

Jack Reeder (9)
Kingscroft Junior School, Staines

Snow Angels

S now is fun
N ow we can play
O n the grass all crunchy
W hite and icy

A nd cold and a blizzard
N o one is sad
G etting snow to make snowmen
E veryone's excited
L ovely clear icicles
S nowballs are fun too.

Lauren Hume (10)
Kingscroft Junior School, Staines

Snow Time

S now is falling to the ground
N ear and far across the land
O ver hilltops, over roofs
W eather has changed, someone's got the flu.

T ime for a snowball fight,
I ndeed it's time to go inside
M rs Barrett's cool as cucumber
E very time I look outside I feel like a snowball fight.

Rebecca Manning (9)
Kingscroft Junior School, Staines

Snow

Skidding through the frosty snow
Falling over as I go
Snowflakes falling on the ground
Making snowmen all around
Snowball fighting everywhere
I feel the breeze in the air.

Chloe Poole (9)
Kingscroft Junior School, Staines

Snow

In the snow I sit and stare
Ice fishing we do out here
Snowball fighting is delighting
Freezing cold in the icing.

Sapphire Meacock (10)
Kingscroft Junior School, Staines

Snowballs

S nowflakes fluttering in the sky.
N o pavement to be seen anywhere.
O ver the world and far away, snow!
W e are having fun in the snow
B eautiful white snow everywhere.
A cross the icy river along the road as we shiver.
L akes, ice, snowballs are fun for everyone.
L ong the road no more snow, but what's this falling from the sky?
Snow! Hooray!

Kelly Smith (9)
Kingscroft Junior School, Staines

The Snow

The snow is falling,
Everyone is laughing with joy.
Megan and Connie are excited
Going skating,
Getting soaked in the snow!

Amber Dickens (10)
Kingscroft Junior School, Staines

The Snow

Snow is falling.
Snow is blowing
And is falling on the ground.
People play in it all day.
Fight in the snow,
Snowball fight.

Billy Rendell (9)
Kingscroft Junior School, Staines

Snow

The snow is falling
People are cooling
Icicles freeze
In the breeze
There are snowball fights
Going on all day and night
Everybody's going to get
Very, very icy and wet
Snow, snow is very fun
Skidding over everyone
It is freezing cold
You're never too old
Snowmen are built
While Scottish play in their kilts
The snow is lovely and white all night.

Connie Stevens (9)
Kingscroft Junior School, Staines

Snowflakes

S nowflakes falling, aren't they pretty?
N othing stopping them swirling round and round.
O h don't they look like stars that are white?
W on't you see them falling to the ground?
F loating gracefully
L eaving the clouds
A nyone will see how many stars in the sky
K indly God has sent the sun to warm us up and spoil the fun.
E nding is this snowy spectacle
S o bye-bye and tomorrow is another day.

Joanna Sutton (9)
Kingscroft Junior School, Staines

Snow

Snow falls down to the ground,
When it touches, not a sound.
Snow is a mystery, when it falls,
Turning things to ice, even walls.
Children playing in the snow,
As it falls, swaying to and fro.
Snowballs are thrown,
From where it's not known.
As they fly onto somebody,
Snow falls down to the ground,
When it touches, not a sound.

Jacob Smith (9)
Kingscroft Junior School, Staines

Snow

Beautiful snow all white and icy
Snow on the ground settling nicely,
Peacefully melting in the sun,
All gone by tomorrow even the fun.
Now nothing to do, no snowball fights,
And back to boring snowless nights.

Sophie Tanner (10)
Kingscroft Junior School, Staines

One Summer Evening

One summer evening,
We heard a sudden knocking.
We opened the door,
To find a pop band rocking.
When they had gone
I heard a scrabbling.
I opened the door to find
To find a mouse having a gnaw.

Isobel Newbury (9)
Meath Green Junior School, Horley

The Top Teacher

I know a teacher that is really top
She is cool and great
I like her very much
Her frizzy hair
Makes people care
But please beware
For when she's angry
She will look at you with a piercing stare
On Fridays though if you're pretty good
You get pops and sweets, *mmm, yum!*
Yes we all like her lots and lots
And when she leaves she will always
Be the tops!

Sophie Buxton (9)
Meath Green Junior School, Horley

The Storm

There was a day when the sky turned black
And the clouds got upset.
It was a day when the lightning god came for revenge.

He boomed! He boomed!
His vicious thunder boomed!
He crashed! He crashed!
His blasting lightning crashed!

His dance of havoc filled the air.
His balls of wind, they blew down houses.
But the final course was to rule the night
With a loud roar and a good night's rest.

Dean Primmer (8)
Meath Green Junior School, Horley

Ice Cream

C hunky
H unks
O f
C hocolate chips
O f
L oveliness
A rriving at my
T ongue,
E ntering now.

I cy and
C reamy,
E at it all up it's

C overed in
R aspberry sauce.
E ating, slurping
A nd I need
M ore!

Elizabeth Cain (11)
Meath Green Junior School, Horley

RNLI

If I get stuck or fall off a boat,
They will help me and I will float,
If I go windsurfing but it gets out of control,
They will lift me up from the goodness of their soul,
If I get in trouble way out at sea,
They will be the ones that rescue me,
So if I'm out there about to die,
I will be saved by the . . .
RNLI.

Cherish Thorpe (8)
Meath Green Junior School, Horley

Vikings

They come in their longboats
With horns like cows,
One falls off every then and now
All armed with axes
They break down the gate,
We all try to run but most are too late.
Destroying all in their path
The Vikings charge in,
Making horrible noises
And a terrible din,
They knock over tables
And smash every plate,
It will not be long until all meet their fate
Now the raiding is over they're all going back,
They chopped off my wrist and they have broken my back
But I know that soon they'll be back for attack!

Eden Medcalf (10)
Meath Green Junior School, Horley

Skate In Tesco

Noseslide, boardslide, kickflip, ollie
Skidding round Tesco on the back of a trolley
Got some wicked new spitfire wheels
And I'm taking out the microwaveable meals
The guard shouts 'Stop!' I act like I don't know what it means
Oh no, I'm gonna crash into a tower of tinned beans
Crash, bang, wallop! Beans everywhere
They're all over me, even in my hair
Next time I go out to buy my mum some pork
I'm not gonna skate
I'm gonna walk!

Callan Howard (10)
Meath Green Junior School, Horley

My Cat

He gazed at me with loving eyes,
Few eyes are that blue,
He had a loud purr,
And a midget mew.

He rubbed himself against the chair,
His looks he should abort,
His hair is fine and ginger,
His fur is very short.

He darts and pats the air,
And why I cannot tell,
He walks, entranced,
At some invisible smell.

He flops down,
With his eyes firmly closed,
And finally goes to sleep,
With one paw on his nose.

Kimberley Allen (11)
Meath Green Junior School, Horley

Teachers!

There is this teacher I really hate,
I'd like to use him as shark bait.
His frizzy hair,
And his frightening stare.
His fingers are all long and bony,
So he doesn't even have one crony.
His aftershave,
Could start a rave.
So if you want a little peer,
I suggest you drink four pints of bitter beer.

Rebecca Connor (9)
Meath Green Junior School, Horley

Fear

Fear is tiny, so small you can fight it.
Fear smells of rotting cheese and sour milk.
It tastes like Brussels sprouts.
Fear doesn't look like anything
Which makes it ever more spooky.

Fear sounds like a floorboard
Creaking and
Your nails scraping down a
Blackboard.
It makes you shudder so badly it is
Almost real, so realistic that you
Jump in fright.

Fear speaks in a low, husky whisper
So quiet that you are not sure he's
There
But he's there alright, his heavy,
Rasping breath
Hot on your cheek!

Laura Tadman (10)
Meath Green Junior School, Horley

The Day The Huts Came Down

The starving metal monster woke up.
Suddenly he remembered his flattened breakfast.
He wanted to crush our hut down.
He staggered over to our hut.
Then he started to destroy us.
He hole punched our bashed wall.
He demolished the chipped door,
He cracked the wrecked lights.
He stomped over to the broken fire exit
And wore out the tired hut.
He destroyed the whole roof into oblivion.

Cameron May (7)
Meath Green Junior School, Horley

I'm Meant To Be Writing A Poem!

I'm meant to be writing a poem,
This girl next to me has done one about a teacher, ahem!
'There is this teacher I really hate,
I'd like to use him as shark bait.'
But Mr Irvine said it has to rhyme all the way through
And apparently it would be hard to do
That all the way through
Her poem,
And I have no idea what to write about,
So unless you want to read about nothing much
I suggest you stop reading.
Yaaawn, it's very boring
I'll have a go,
Ineey-meenee-minee-mo
Santa Claus says, 'Ho, ho, ho!'
Ok, so that was dumb, but I tried.
Oh dear, I ran out of time, I am being sarcastic
Bye, see ya, bye, is everybody gone? Huh?

Rebecca Inman (9)
Meath Green Junior School, Horley

Aliens! Aliens!

Aaahhh! Aliens are invading
Run aaahhh!

Martians are invading with their
UFOs attacking with giant laser guns.

Aliens come in shapes and sizes,
Some can be green
And some can come out of the garbage can,
And some can have big heads and antennas.

Aliens' planets are so cool
I wish I was an alien living on Mars
Aliens aaahhh!

Jack Kidd (9)
Meath Green Junior School, Horley

Leaves

See all the colours of the leaves,
Floating from the trees to the ground
They come in red, yellow, brown and gold
In autumn is when this happens,
Along with conkers and nuts.

But in spring and summer
The leaves will turn to green,
They can be circle or square,
They could be big or small.

You can find them in China or in Jamaica
They might be on the ground or on a bush or tree
They are used for many reasons like eating or cleaning
So watch out for the leaves they may inspire you!

Liberty Hill (9)
Meath Green Junior School, Horley

Road Rage

Swing open the door,
Hop right in,
Turn the ignition and let the engine ring!
Push down forcefully,
Skid off and have a laugh,
Show off with a wheelie!
Speed down the interstate,
You know at the traffic lights,
You should wait,
But you don't care,
Because down the motorway you tear!
Racing cars,
Because it's *road rage!*

David Fletcher (10)
Meath Green Junior School, Horley

The Last Wicket

Down to the last pair of batsman.
The atmosphere was tense,
The opposition only needed three runs to win.
I rubbed the ball for luck
Focused on the wicket with victory in my sight,
Ran and bowled with all my might.
Our team held their breath.
The ball flew straight as an arrow.
The batsman stood ready,
He swung and missed.
Our team jumped for joy,
And *'Howzat'* was the triumphant cry,
As the ball spun through the air,
Bounced and made that bale fly.

Callum Ross-Freeman (10)
Meath Green Junior School, Horley

The Thing

Beware of the thing

The thing is out to get you
He will make no sight or
Sneeze
He will follow you everywhere
Even in the chilly breeze

Beware of the thing

He has fur as bright as moonlight
Eyes glint in the moonlight
He will only come out at moonlight

Beware of the thing.

Catherine Fuller (9)
Meath Green Junior School, Horley

Dream Castle

There is a castle in my dreams
That isn't really what it seems.
It's grey, though it may not seem that way,
And all you ever do is play.

It's really big and hard to get to
But here's the secret the journey won't hurt you.
And if you're wondering where it is
It's at a place owned by Liz.

It's a cloud where this castle is built
And Liz is the angel in a green kilt.
When you get there (if you do)
All the birds will start to coo.

The birds you get there are phoenixes and kiwi
And I know a friend of Liz, that's me!
There are lots of angels up there on the cloud
Oh! And don't forget boys aren't allowed.

Inside the castle are lots of toys
And they can't be ruined by lots of boys.
There are forty-nine rooms full of girls
And one jewellery room packed with pearls.

The name of the castle is unknown
But there's no reason that you should moan.
The people there are very nice
But don't worry there isn't a price.

How to get there that's what you want to know
Just close your eyes and say you want to go.
And before you know it you'll be having lots of fun
Playing in the castle and the bright warm sun!

Esther Nye (9)
Meath Green Junior School, Horley

Tiff

Handling well through corners,
With Tiff Nedell at the wheel,
He crashes through a boathouse,
But my God he won't pay the bill!

Skidding onto the racetrack,
He roars past the line,
Beating the other drivers,
But cutting it very fine.

Now he's on the motorway,
And revving the engine fast,
The toll-station is completely empty,
But they don't see him screech past!

Over the bridge he goes,
But it's going up, oh no!
He keeps on going like a rocket,
Now there's a fearsome foe!

But he finally sees his opponent,
When Vicky is spotted ahead,
She thinks she can beat him,
But her car's made of lead!

Ben Tadman (11)
Meath Green Junior School, Horley

The Magic Box

(Based on 'Magic Box' by Kit Wright)

I will put in the box . . .
A splash of a dolphin's tail
Cat swimming water
Two tortoises twiddling tails.

I will put in the box . . .
A first giggle from a child's lips
A last cry from a sabre-toothed tiger
Nine naughty negative knights.

I will put in the box . . .
An alien walking on the seabed
And a horse on a rocket
Seven silky snails skiving in the air.

I will put in the box . . .
An ice cream frozen in the sun
A rabbit as strong as an ox
Eight elephants eating exciting eggs.

My box is made from . . .
Flittering crystals from the highest mountains
There are secrets in the corners,
The hinges are made from a devil's tail
The lid is made from pure sapphire sparkling in the sunlight.

Tiffany Marshall (9)
Minster CE Primary School, Ramsgate

The Magic Box

(Based on 'Magic Box' by Kit Wright)

I will put in my box . . .
A balloon touching a space comet
Sparkling stars coming up from Earth
Raspberries that never go out of date

I will put in the box . . .
A submarine up in space
A nosey nose sniffing about
A piece of golden hair from Goldilocks.

I will put in the box . . .
A swishing of a mermaid's tail
A swimming cat and a walking shark
A fish that knows everything.

I will put in the box . . .
Some jewellery from days gone by
A rainbow with odd colours like shin and dark brown
And a talking picture.

My box is made from a filled love heart,
In the corners I'll have Discos, drinks, sweets and salad,
Butterfly wings for the hinges
On my lid multicoloured fairy dust from Tinkerbelle.

I shall be a helpful zookeeper
Keeping spiders to elephants and buzzy bees
I'll be as kind in my box with glee.

Jessica McDougall (8)
Minster CE Primary School, Ramsgate

The Magic Box

(Based on 'Magic Box' by Kit Wright)

I will put in the box . . .
A flying mouse and a walking aeroplane,
The wing of a dragon, beating as it flies.

I will put in the box . . .
An exciting school and a boring holiday,
A sword with a handle of gold and ice.

I will put in the box . . .
The first bite of an Indian feast,
The last laugh of an old grandpa
A golden hair from a dancing tiger.

I will put in the box . . .
A silver scale of a slithering snake,
The claw of a tiger,
And the roar of an angry lion.

My box is made from . . .
The most shiny pearl from the bottom of the ocean
With excitement hiding in the corners
And the hinges are made from dragon's claws.

Toby Allen (9)
Minster CE Primary School, Ramsgate

The Magic Box
(Based on 'Magic Box' by Kit Wright)

I shall put in the box . . .
The tooth of an ancient dinosaur,
The claw of a young child,
And the cosy armchair of my past.

I shall put in the box . . .
The chocolate brown rainbow,
And the rainbow coloured dog,
With a pop star from Portugal.

I shall put in the box . . .
The first squeak of a newborn mouse,
The loudest scream of a baby,
And a diamond from the longest tunnel.

My box is made from . . .
Thousands of tiny glinting scales gleaming in the light
The corners are filled with the latest secrets
And the hinges are mauve petals holding on tightly!

I shall dive in the ocean with the giant whales by my side,
Then I shall ride on a dolphin till the weather gets wild!

Lauren Peall (8)
Minster CE Primary School, Ramsgate

The Magic Box
(Based on 'Magic Box' by Kit Wright)

My magic box will have . . .
A swish of a hot wave making its way to shore
A flying cat and a walking bat.

My magic box will have . . .
A canter of a white horse and the walk of a pony
A portrait of my mother and an x-ray of my brother.

My magic box will have . . .
A teddy bear with eyes like crystals
And a pink and white gun full of marshmallows.

My magic box will have . . .
Some perfect pearls and some shiny shells
A beautiful coloured rainbow with gold and silver at the end.

My magic box is made from . . .
A beautiful pink patch of unicorn's skin
The hinges are golden feathers from a beautiful bird.
A sparkling rope from a whirling, twirling whirlwind
And don't forget the stuff inside a gleaming crystal and a mini slide.

I shall . . .
Sail across the ocean and sail across the sea
And ride a pink dolphin in my box
And meet the loch Ness monster
And wash ashore a beautiful yellow beach.

Abby Wilkinson (9)
Minster CE Primary School, Ramsgate

The Magic Box Poem

(Based on 'Magic Box' by Kit Wright)

I will put in my box . . .
A dragon tinkling sweetly as it hangs from the low ceiling of a cottage
Wind chimes roaring as they fly above the fluffy clouds
The bounce of Tigger jumping through the thick trees.

I will put in my box . . .
The gentle swish of a dolphin's fin
The flapping wings of a beautiful sparrow
The sound of electricity flowing through a wire.

I will put in the box . . .
The glittering horn of a snow-white unicorn
The first cry of a newborn baby
And the final wrap of the last mummy's bandages.

I will put in the box . . .
Every animal there is on Earth, big, small, ugly and beautiful
The soar of an old golden eagle
The shimmer of a slithery snake shining in the sun.

My box is made from . . .
The most glittery crystals you can ever find
The imaginative dreams of young children hide in the corners
The hinges will be the big, bright and colourful wings of butterflies
And the lid shall be made of rosy red rubies and bright
blue sapphires.

I shall . . .
Dive with swift dolphins to the bottom of the deep, blue ocean
And on the way down
I will meet Dory the tong fish from Finding Nemo.

Chloe Bennett (9)
Minster CE Primary School, Ramsgate

The Magic Box

(Based on 'Magic Box' by Kit Wright)

I will put in the box . . .
The wink of a horse's eye
A spark of fairy dust,
The world touching the tip of my finger.

I will put in the box . . .
A friendly, cheetah sitting on my lap,
A vicious cat hunting for food,
A hair from an old grandpa's beard.

I will put in the box . . .
A swish of water from the Atlantic
The first fine shimmer of a fish's scale
The last laugh of a great hyena.

I will put in the box . . .
A bushy fox's tail
A floppy rabbit's long ear
A giraffe's long dainty neck.

My box is made from . . .
Finest grape vines in the country
The hinges are made of crabs claws
The lid has grapes hanging from it.

I shall . . .
Ride a great white horse to a land far away
And chat to the twinkling fairies
And swim with dolphins.

Lauren Hockey (9)
Minster CE Primary School, Ramsgate

The Magic Box

(Based on 'Magic Box' by Kit Wright)

I will put in my box . . .
The first growl of a baby lion
The last cry of a caveman
The first explosion of a star.

I will put in my box . . .
The last blink of a suffering cat
The first growing wing of a bird
The last bite of a shark.

I will put in my box . . .
The first hand lighting of God
The last meeting of Jesus
The first joke in the world.

I will put in my box . . .
Seven sharks swimming
A thirteenth month
And a red moon.

My box is made from . . .
Ice and gold with a sun in the middle and thoughts in the side
The hinges are made from sharks' teeth.

I shall . . .
Climb Mount Everest and sleep there for the night
And in the morning I will go snowboarding down it.

Ashley Hill (9)
Minster CE Primary School, Ramsgate

The Magic Box

(Based on 'Magic Box' by Kit Wright)

I will put in my box . . .
The birth of a baby cat
And the death of an ancient dinosaur
The glowing of a human heart

I will put in my box . . .
The stillness of a cat
The pounding of a human heart
And the brightness of a star.

I will put in my box . . .
A slimy snail slid down a slope
Two tiny tigers trying to sleep
And one grizzly gorilla.

I will put in my box . . .
A cat that needed a nap
Eight tiny teddy bears sipping some tea.

I will put in my box . . .
The lid's made from silky bird feathers
The hinges are made from butterfly wings,
The corners have got some secrets never to be told

I shall ride on a dolphin under the Indian Ocean.

Ellen Holland (9)
Minster CE Primary School, Ramsgate

The Magic Box

(Based on 'Magic Box' by Kit Wright)

I will put in the box . . .
A yellow shark with arms and legs
And a man with a tail and fins
Seven slippery snakes slithering on the seashore.

I will put in the box . . .
Eight apples black and white
Two cats red and green
And a fat lady upside down.

I will put in the box . . .
A melting glacier and a frozen sun
My mum's first baby and my dad's eldest brother.

I will put in the box . . .
Five foxes fishing for fish
Eight rabbits hunting for foxes
And a dog with green frogs legs.

My box is made from . . .
Glittering ice crystals
The hinges are sharp claws from cat paws
The lid is covered in royal red petals,
I shall swim in and out of the waves on a dolphin's back and
I shall fight with a tiger,
I shall swim with peace and quiet.

Hannah Jackson (9)
Minster CE Primary School, Ramsgate

Sisters

I hate sisters they shout too much
Huffy, puffy everywhere.
Annoying and shouty.
Teenagers have moody days.
Enormous mess in the bathroom.
Sorting their make-up and their hair
Icing cakes and eating them all.
Standing in the way of the TV.
Talking too loud.
Everywhere they have to fuss, fuss, fuss.
Running up and down.
Enormous make-up on the floor.
Standing up for each other sometimes.

Albertina Marfo-Mensah (10)
St James The Great Primary School, Thornton Heath

Dolphins Play

Dolphins play in the deep blue sea on and on they go,
Laughing, jumping having fun proudly moving to and fro,
But now the day has come to the end
Dolphins say goodbye to their friends.
A new day has become
So let's all say we're having fun
Running up and down the beach
But now the sun is out of reach
Again and again we say goodbye
And hope in the future the sun is in the sky.

Catherine Onoselase (10)
St James The Great Primary School, Thornton Heath

Market

Is everyone driving you round the bend?
From the friendship shop, you can buy a friend.

Is everyone moaning, 'bout your smelly feet
Buy a nice clean one and get one free!

Come to us, if your plants have died,
We'll plan a funeral, to say bye-bye!

If you have a broken arm, go to the second-hand shop,
I give you my advice; they sell quite a lot!

Do you need veg, cabbage or leeks?
Also cheese and eggs, going cheap! Cheap!

Training your baby, to go to the loo
Go to the pottery shop and ask for a potty or two.

Come, if your computer has gone haywire,
I'll remove the hay; it will take a while.

Is your disc or CD still not working?
We'll find it a job, if it would stop talking!

Come to us, we sell everything here,
You are deaf! I'll lend you an ear!

Rosalind de Souza (9)
St James The Great Primary School, Thornton Heath

London Express

The London Express is on its way to the row of time.
The people on it were frightened by the sound of a chime.
The time just passes by the window with a quiet tick-tock.
The wind whooshing by the train is it, or is it just the lock?
The time, the chime, the quiet tick-tock, the lock and the silence.
Stopped clock.

Patsy Dixon (9)
St James The Great Primary School, Thornton Heath

Sports

Sports are fun
Sports are great
Sports are things
You'll never hate.

I like sports
There are lots to do
But you can't do them
If you've got the flu.

Sports are nice
And very cool
You can do some
In a swimming pool.

Sports are enjoyable
They are really nice
And thankfully they don't
Involve any mice!

Hannah Stock (9)
St James The Great Primary School, Thornton Heath

Midnight

Darkness fills the night
The lamps bare their yellow teeth with light,
The wind whistles a harsh breeze
Not a sound - not even a sneeze.

Stars glow in the midnight
Only revealing little light
Morning, morning still to come
But midnight still beats like a drum.

Denice Koduah (11)
St James The Great Primary School, Thornton Heath

Zoo

Monkeys are bad
And are very mad
Penguins are cool
Because they live in a pool.

Giraffes are tall
And they can't sit on a stool
They get to eat food that is cool
They want to live in a pool.

Lions are wild
And roar at a child
Elephants eat grass
But I've never seen them walk past.

Dolphins are sweet
You can't have them to eat
Seals are fat
And they never wear a hat.

Kristina Lucia (8)
St James The Great Primary School, Thornton Heath

Danielle

D reamy, well kind of,
A dvanced, you can say that again.
N eeds to be asked twice, never!
I mpossible, that really is impossible.
E nthusiastic, of course,
L oves poems, absolutely right.
L ilac is her favourite colour, true blue,
E nd, I'm afraid that's true.

Danielle D'Cruz (8)
St James The Great Primary School, Thornton Heath

Animal Madness

There's animals all over the house,
From the largest elephant
Down to the smallest mouse,
Mum's screaming and jumping on a chair,
Dad's getting angry and ripping out his hair,
My sisters are chasing dogs everywhere,
Dad's getting more angry and ripping out more hair.
Meanwhile I'm on my bed stroking a lizard,
All these animals my brains in a blizzard.
When I'm older, I may buy a zoo,
Oh no! Mum's calling me,
Her face has turned blue!
She may feel sick!
Dad's still chasing the dogs, while screaming!
'When I catch you, I'll give you a hard kick!'
It's animal madness in my house,
From the largest elephant,
To smallest mouse!

Joanna D'Cruz (11)
St James The Great Primary School, Thornton Heath

Can I Have A Pet?

'I really, really want a pet'
My mum says 'No!'
'But can't I? Can't I just get
A monkey called Joe?'

'No!' says Mum, 'No!' says Mum.
'What will we feed him?'
'They're not small, silly or dumb,
Just very trim!'

'I will' I said, 'I will,
He can sleep with me
And eat bananas I will grill
For breakfast, lunch and tea.'

Kathleen Lissenburg (9)
St James The Great Primary School, Thornton Heath

Sara Corvaglia

S ensible
A lter server
R eally good at Irish dancing
A ctive

C harming
O rganised
R eally good at giving advice
V ery caring
A dorable
G ood at making friends
L ilac is the colour of my bedroom
I ntelligent
A lways helps other people.

Sara Corvaglia (8)
St James The Great Primary School, Thornton Heath

The Sound Of Summer

(Inspired by 'Goldfish' by Henri Matisse)

In comes the waking dawn
Slowly rising shining bright,
The creatures of day start to rise
One of them flies to me with rapid flight.

The sound of water and four fish
Desperate to join the others,
And regain swimming in happiness,
The sound and colours of animals, flowers and trees.

The night draws on, the creatures disappear,
The flowers disappear and sink into the ground,
The water shakes, the fish take rest,
The water silences waiting for dawn.

David Drewitt (10)
St Stephen's Primary School, Welling

The Whirlpool Of Feeling
(Inspired by 'The Scream' by Edvard Munch)

Colours mixed together, to paint a haunted scene,
Mixed together, to form a whirlpool of feelings.

A bridge formed by sadness,
And the gentle waves mixed up, and confused.

The sky filled with happiness, like an angels delight.

An island of a few people,
The air filled with worries,
As the colours bind together,
Together like a rainbow in a mess.

Fall together to make a whirlpool of feelings.
But eventually the whirlpool of feelings dies down.

Robyn Ryan (11)
St Stephen's Primary School, Welling

The Tilled Field
(Inspired by 'The Tilled Field' by Joan Miró)

There's a tail of a horse and a dragon's head
Below a sky of yellow and a night of red
Stranger and stranger are the eyes in trees
With spiky dogs and saffron seas.

A Torah and a chicken with legs of jade
And an eel in a tube that's getting paid.

Fields of orange and half a cow
Follow the wire up to a house.

It looks so happy with colours bright
But you're only looking through tainted light.

Lucinda Smith (10)
St Stephen's Primary School, Welling

The Funny Poem

(Inspired by 'The Scream' by Edvard Munch)

Air filled with funny colours.
Funny laughter,
Funny things.

Light colours,
Dark colours,
Medium colours,
What do you think?

Colours are flowing,
Waves of orange crimson and buff,
Twisted colours of indigo and lavender,
A dash of chestnut.

A splash of green,
Distorted faces everywhere,
Sweep of brown,
Amber swirls.

Lucy Buss (11)
St Stephen's Primary School, Welling

The Bog Land

Slippery, sloppery, slippery, slap,
Attached to a toboggan by a strap,
Many bears have lost their lives,
Looking for yellow beehives.

I found myself surrounded by mire,
My brother and sister are liars,
For they told me I would not sink,
In this mud that looks like ink.

George Priddle (10)
St Stephen's Primary School, Welling

A Lonely Heart

(Inspired by 'Forest And Dove' by Max Ernest)

No movement, standing still
Perch upon a branch of tree
Safe from kill
Is this bird a he or she?
It doesn't matter

Trees of bad
Staring up
Trees of mad
Nothing as nice as a baby pup
It's a sign of death

The bird colour of red
Trees of daring brown
And now the bird is dead
Looking down
Until it starts again.

Tina Hopkins (10)
St Stephen's Primary School, Welling

The Castle

In the times that have past
When knights were bold in their task
And castles spread across the land
Passed down hand by hand
Some were owned by kings and queens
Or noblemen strong and mean
Some will go and some will stay
Right until the present day
Tonbridge Castle moved from high to low
Hastings Castle was knocked down in a blow.

Richard Holbrow (10)
St Stephen's Primary School, Welling

Seaport

(Inspired by 'Seaport with Embarkation of Saint Ursula' by Claude Lorraine)

Around the seaport the tiny boats ran,
Shouts and cries came from each man,
She laid down her anchor, the mother of ships,
A sailor takes ropes from her side, to the quay he clips.

Huge boats washed water up to the shore,
There on the ships, vanilla, indigo and lemon flags did soar,
The streets were filled with mindless chatter,
None of which had any matter.

Down the sun went, lower and lower,
An oar out of time from one tired rower,
The tiny boats dotted around,
Glided over the ripples without making a sound.

This busy seaport goes to sleep each night,
But at dawn each day it is launched back into flight.

Emma Wilson (10)
St Stephen's Primary School, Welling

Deception

(Inspired by 'The Tilled Field' by Joan Miró)

Calm mellow, land of tranquillity
Dream world and fantasy.
But look closer, in more detail,
Look down to the very depths.

Trees with eyes that see, you see where you are going.
Oh look a horse, a horse but wait, fangs on an evil face.
A chicken with two scarlet legs, a bird with horns upon his head
If it was there I would have fled.

Slugs slip by and spiders screech
All around yellow sand like from a beach
Then from the corner of this scene creeps nightfall
Blood dripping from its seams!

Charlotte Tringham (11)
St Stephen's Primary School, Welling

The Shark

(Inspired by 'The Physical Impossibility of Death in the Mind of Someone Living (Shark)' by Damien Hirst)

One long tank, in a big empty room,
A wave of blue and green water,
In it something dead and still, no life at all.
Creepy, very creepy,
Did you just see it move?
Or was it just your imagination?

Go into the room with a tourist group.
Hear all of the information,
The group goes, leaving you behind,
Then it's just you and him.
You stare at him, he stares at you
With his piercing black eyes.
Who is going to win?
One more second, you can't bear it.
You run out of the empty room.
It has won, the shark.

Creepy, very creepy!

Natasha Turner (10)
St Stephen's Primary School, Welling

The Polobug

There was once a Polobug,
That polobugged around,
It is said he balanced on one foot,
And lived in a dirt mound.

Many think his body was green,
And covered in silver stars,
No one knew from where he came,
Did he come from China or Mars?

Did the Polobug have many eyes?
Or was he very hairy?
Was his nose pointed?
Or did he dress up as a fairy?

Could the Polobug read or write?
Did he have a brain?
Was he very fancy?
Or was he rather plain?

So if you see this creature,
Ask him what you may,
But make sure to be cautious,
In what you do and say!

Kate Mythen (10)
St Stephen's Primary School, Welling

The Niagara Falls

(Inspired by 'Niagara Falls' painted by Church)

Rivers crash down the cliffs
And make a fresh new start,
Far as the eye can see
Time for the fish to part.

Down by the sharp, sprayed rocks
A small rainbow appears,
Streaks of coloured flowers,
Over the river's tears.

Over in the distance
Close by the riverbank,
Forests lay in great health,
Near where the river sank.

All the crashing views,
And the striking colours,
And forests lush and green,
Keep the place peaceful and
The rivers pure and clean.

Jack Goodwin (11)
St Stephen's Primary School, Welling

I'd Love To Be A Pen

I'd love to be a pen,
And do what I want to do,
I'd never have to go and learn,
Or dress up for a do!

I'd always get lots of exercise,
Without even moving myself a bit,
I wouldn't have to worry about doctors,
Or having a laughter fit!

For once I would be able to use my mouth,
And not be told to zip it up,
My mouth would be the pen top,
So my head would not imitate a cup!

But after a very hard days work,
I'd be put back into the pen pot,
With all my brothers and sisters and cousins,
And we'd talk about gossip and rumours, the lot!

Thomas Gardner (11)
St Stephen's Primary School, Welling

Friends

Friends are nice, friends are kind
Friends are nice to be around.

No matter how we argue or fight
I know we'll always be all right.

We share our secrets and our fun,
Together we laugh and run.

April Freeland (10)
South Farnham Junior School, Farnham

Animals

Animals, animals all around
Animals, animals can astound!
In the jungle, up a tree,
Almost everywhere you can see!

Animals, animals in the park,
Two by two heading to the ark!
Elephants, monkeys, giraffes and birds,
Antelope and rhinos both come in herds!

Animals, animals in the sea,
Animals, animals jumping on me!
Splishing, splashing, having fun,
Then the big blue whale, which weighs a tonne!

Animals, animals under the ground,
Animals, animals which don't make a sound!
Minibeasts, minibeasts, some with wings,
Animals are definitely my favourite things!

David Parry (11)
South Farnham Junior School, Farnham

Friends

Friends are nice, friends are lovely,
They cheer me up when I'm sad or lonely,
They make me smile when I am with them,
And I'm always glad to see them,
We laugh all day and have lots of fun!
Until the day is over and night suddenly comes,
Friends are always there for you,
Even if you're feeling blue,
Come along and you will see,
That all my friends are here for me!

Marion Dale (11)
South Farnham Junior School, Farnham

Dizzy

Dizzy is my puppy
She has ears like velvet
Her fur is soft and fluffy
Her cold wet nose is like a button
She looks at me with her beautiful eyes like melted chocolate.

Dizzy is my puppy
She runs around like a whirlwind
Being energetic she needs lots of exercise
Dizzy loves to play with dogs
But chases horses even though they must seem like elephants
She thinks she can fly because she jumps like a squirrel.

Dizzy is my puppy
I am very proud when she learns new tricks
Sometimes she makes me angry when she tries to bite
The best thing about Dizzy is she is always happy to see me
I love her all over.

James Rigg (10)
South Farnham Junior School, Farnham

Alien Friends

Once I met an alien from outer space,
I named him Zog and he had a weird face.

Zog had a mechanical dog called Ace,
They seemed quite friendly so they stayed at my place.

Zog and Ace my two new friends,
Drove Mum and Dad right round the bend!

They told them to go but the aliens wouldn't listen,
So I sent them off on another space mission.

I was very sad to see them go,
I hope they drop by again to say hello.

Harry Carter (10)
South Farnham Junior School, Farnham

On Your Marks

To the whipping area I am called
Some children big and some are small.
A bundle of boys await the sign
To go up to the blocks - it's time, it's time.

I walk up slowly - getting scared
Hearts apounding, not aware
Of people shouting, 'Come on Will,
You can do it, show your skill!'

And then silence.

The starter gets out his starting gun
And raises it - here comes the fun.
'On your marks' he says aloud
Down I bend and await the sound.

Of the *'Bang!'*

Blasting forward - reaching out
I dive in far - 'Come on' they shout.
Kicking legs and powering arms,
Pulling water, feeling calm.

And then the turn.

The end of the pool - a tumble turn
It's now my muscles start to burn.
But now I'm going really fast,
No one can reach me or get past.

Or will they?

The last few metres feel so good,
I feel relaxed, I know I should.
I hit the wall - the end has come,
The crowd is cheering, the race is done.

William Miller (10)
South Farnham Junior School, Farnham

The Series Of Unfortunate Events Poem

(Based on 'A series of Unfortunate Events' by Daniel Handler)

I'm going to tell you a story full of misfortune and despair,
Horrid, disgusting descriptions which will make you rip
out your hair.
For three Baudelaire orphans, their hearts were full of woe,
When the news of the fire was delivered by the banker Mr Poe.
Violet would invent things, while Klaus would just read,
Sunny would bite hard objects in her hour of need.
But then they got sent to a man whose name was Count Olaf,
And it wasn't just his clothes that were to say the least quite naff.
He was an evil man and extremely mean,
And he had plotted a really monstrous scheme.
He planned to steal the Baudelaire money,
All of it from Violet, Klaus and Sunny.
This is when the trouble really began,
It was up to them to stop this awful wicked plan.
But Count Olaf had assistants, full of terror and spite,
You could see they were loaded with greed at first sight.
There was the hook-handed man,
And a bald guy with a huge nose span.
A person who looked neither male nor female,
And two ladies that looked sooo pale.
They threatened the children and drank lots of wine,
Each one was ready to commit lots of crime.
The Baudelaires didn't like Olaf and his nasty house,
But they liked his neighbour Justice Strauss.
Count Olaf had one eyebrow and on his ankle a tattoo of an eye,
Which would haunt the Baudelaires forever and that's no lie.
I'm not going to ruin it for people who have yet to read the story
So all I'll say is this time Olaf's plan did not bring him glory
So Count Olaf did not succeed, well not yet anyway,
But thoughts of him remain in the Baudelaires' brains every day.
You shouldn't have read this poem, if scared of murder,
blood and gore,
But however much you fear, remember the Baudelaires' fear
much more!

Beth O'Dell (11)
South Farnham Junior School, Farnham

I Don't Care What People Say, If You Do You Have To Pay

Whether people think I'm thin or if they think I'm fat
People must be stupid if they think I go lower than that.

I don't care what people say,
If you do you have to pay.

I know that if my presence is needed
I don't always need to be pleaded!

I don't care what people say,
If you do you have to pay.

I think that I can sing, I love it, I love it, it's my favourite thing,
If you don't or if you do I won't ever make you.

I don't care what people say,
If you do you have to pay.

Sarah Zeiher (11)
South Farnham Junior School, Farnham

Africa

Whilst a terrible tiger tossed his tangled tail,
A leaping lion lost his lovely lioness,
A rampaging rhino roamed round the ragged rocks,
A mischievous monkey meandered madly over the melon,
A friendly fish friskily froze when seeing a friendly face,
A silvery snake slithered down the slippery slope,
A crafty croc crept through the cramped crater,
A galloping gazelle galloped gleefully over green grass,
A secretive special cat stood in serene splendour,
A wicked warthog whinged and whined while waffling waffles,
And a mangy merekat moaned menacingly at the moon,
I lay in bed dreaming of Africa.

Jonathan Palmer (11)
South Farnham Junior School, Farnham

My Haunted Poem

I'm walking through the woods at night
Underneath the shining moonlight
My hands and feet as cold as ice
As you meet some horrible mice
I'm finally inside the dreadful house at this dreaded time
My heart is pumping madly, is this a crime?
As I tiptoe up the stairs
All my legs and all my hairs
All the cries of the night are heard by every moth,
And as I walk into the room I had a tickly cough
Then suddenly I hear a voice it's coming from the bed
I'm not going in to have a look but this is what it said
'Grizzly ghouls from every tomb
Are closing in to seal your doom
Although you try to stay alive
Your body starts to quiver
And as you walk into the room
You'll soon get a quiver
And as you try to run away
Listen to what we say'
I'm running out the room and what do I see?
A little boy inside a picture, argh! It's me!

Henry Dyne (11)
South Farnham Junior School, Farnham

The Rainbow

R ain through the sun
A rc of colour in the sky
I n mid-air above the city
N ewly born sky after the rain has died out
B ouncing raindrops start to fall
O pen the window for a better view
W here does it go? Will we ever know?

Alastair Hunt (10)
South Farnham Junior School, Farnham

Ball Games

White ball against blue sky,
Watch it fly, fly, fly.

Ball squirting out of the scrum,
Into Jonny's hands!

Disappearing ball into the pocket,
An assortment of colours.

Net bulging, like a billowing sail,
Keeper stranded, crowd roaring.

Henman Hill packed with people,
Big screen showing ace down the line.

Hard ball bouncing, bat flaying,
Wickets rattled, bails sailing.

Strike 3, curve ball,
Home run diamonds flashing.

Bouncing, rolling, looping, curving,
Sliding, soaring, screaming, swerving,
Everyone loves ball games!

Sam England (10)
South Farnham Junior School, Farnham

Heaven On Earth

A world full of chocolate
Made out of chocolate.
Chocolate houses, chocolate trees
Chocolate bars and chocolate seas.
Warm, comforting and happy.

The cocoa bean - who could know
What mysteries this precious fruit holds.
Smooth and silky,
Heavenly and milky,
This brown luxurious treasure.

Lydia Skuse (11)
South Farnham Junior School, Farnham

Seasons Go Round

S ubtle and welcome changes after cold,
P ink and red are the colours of the sun.
R un about and have a play,
I n the garden roll around.
N ever let the sun set,
G o and see the baby lambs.

S un is shining all the day,
U nder umbrellas seeking shade.
M any people like to stay out late,
M ost children are bronzed and lean.
E veryone loves the summer sun,
R oll around and have fun.

A ll the summer sun is moving on,
U nder a nice warm roof you should stay.
T rees are melting you could say,
U nder raincoats children shout.
M any leaves are flying about,
N umerous colours like rainbows are out.

W ind is up and roaring about,
I nside fireplaces glow day and night.
N ight is long and light is short,
T rees are all bare.
E verywhere I look I see white,
R ituals like Christmas make winter cool!

Elizabeth Britchford (10)
South Farnham Junior School, Farnham

My Family

My sister is like the ogre from Shrek,
Bathes in mud, dances around like an elephant,
Thud, thud, thud, like a monster in the morning.
Very scary, for all you out there, warning!
She's a green, mean, fighting machine.
However, she is very angry in the morning
And laughs like a witch to scare you all.
My mother wakes up in the morning and
Hears my sister snoring in the morning.
Like a mouse squeaking when she is snoring.
My sister's on the phone twenty-four-seven because it feels like that.
My brother and me fight every night
With my sister on my arm biting me!
I love them to bits so it's fair.

Ellie Rhodes (10)
South Farnham Junior School, Farnham

Haunted House

Our house is haunted all the way through,
You come to a light, what do you do?
Do you scream?
Or stay and fight?
No way! You know the light is much too bright.
Do you run?
No! The light catches in the sun.

Our house is haunted all the way through,
You come to a clock, what do you do?
Do you swim all the way to the dock?
No way! The clock keeps going tick-tock.
Do you run?
No! Time will catch you in the sun!

Oscar Goode (10)
South Farnham Junior School, Farnham

Christmas Day

When I woke up my mum and dad are still asleep,
So I went around the corner for a peep,
I saw the tree so bright,
Then on my hand I felt something tight,
It was my little brother
That just woke up my mother,
I opened my present it was a surprise
I couldn't believe my eyes
There was lots of holly
Then I saw my friend Polly
Then my grandma and grandad came over
And they gave me a pullover
We took the dog for a walk
Then we had a long talk
So I hope you enjoyed your day.

Chanel Eldridge (11)
South Farnham Junior School, Farnham

The Lion

The lion prowling through the jungle,
Now and then giving a loud roar!
Who might he find for his meal today,
But the one and only boar!

The lion is hiding in the grass;
Ready to pounce on his juicy prey.
Licking his lips as he watches it lying,
He's found his lunch, hooray!

The lion approaches his feast with pleasure;
He bites its neck and begins to tear.
His greedy eyes beaming with joy;
My advice is to be aware!

Kate Rhidian
South Farnham Junior School, Farnham

Maths

I hate maths,
I hate SATs
What are they both?
Maths.

In class I find it boring,
Next you find me snoring,
When we do our tables,
I would rather do the fables.

I think maths is a waste of time,
I would rather stay at home,
Have a party, drink some wine.

Maths makes me sick,
If only I could pick.

I would rather do literacy than maths,
And would rather do geography than stupid SATs.

April Caplin (11)
South Farnham Junior School, Farnham

My Rabbit

My rabbit is called Toffee
She's really rather cute
She lives with her brother bunny

For them seems to suit
Their home is a cage
At the top of our stairs

House rabbits we've they are all the rage
They seem much happier living in pairs
Toffee's fur is soft and fluffy
Her nose twitches and with her brother she will prance

With my mum to music she will dance
She kisses me everywhere
She is really like a small fluffy bear.

Alice Hayes (11)
South Farnham Junior School, Farnham

The Man With The Gun

There was a foolish man with a gun
Who shot an animal just for fun
He picked it up and it weighed a ton
But he didn't regret what he had done.

The animal was a chimpanzee
Who managed to run free after being shot in the arm
It hid and remained calm
The man walked right past it
And tripped over a thick long root out of the ground
This made a very loud sound.

The man was stupid and had a little fall
And then he fell down a waterfall which was very tall
The chimpanzee was happy
And went home to heal his arm and relax in the sun
And that's the end of the man with the gun!

Morgan Owen (10)
South Farnham Junior School, Farnham

PlayStation 2

The PlayStation is my favourite toy,
Whenever I play, it brings me joy.
I normally play it when I get home,
Sometimes it makes my mum and dad moan.

My favourite game is Hit And Run,
Because it features The Simpsons.
Homer and Bart are the stars of the game,
Marge and Lisa are still in the frame.

The aim of the game is to complete
your mission in order,
When this is done you move forward one.
So drop that doughnut and grab the wheel!
It's time to make steal.

Jake Whitear (11)
South Farnham Junior School, Farnham

Animals

A is for animals that walk the Earth,
B is for bats that fly through the night,
C is for cats that are cute and cuddly,
D is for dogs like my pet Halle,
E is for elephants that are big and strong,
F is for frogs that jump from a pond,
G is for giraffes that eat the highest branches,
H is for horses that gallop in a field,
I is for insects that creep and crawl,
J is for jaguars that are the fastest creatures on Earth,
K is for killer whales that live in the deep sea,
L is for lambs that live on a farm,
M is for monkeys that swing through the trees,
N is for nanny goats that my grandad used to keep,
O is for octopus that have eight legs,
P is for pigs that feed from a trough,
Q is for quick hares that run everywhere,
R is for rabbits that graze in a field,
S is for snakes that slither around,
T is for tigers that run in the wild,
U is for unicorn that unusual horse,
V is for voles that my cats like to catch,
W is for wolf the leader of the pack,
X is for extinct those prehistoric dinosaurs,
Y is for yeti that live in the Himalayas,
Z is for zebra that have black and white strips.

Rebekah Wooff (11)
South Farnham Junior School, Farnham

Love

There are many different kinds of love
And one is family love
I love my family, they are so nice to me,
When I'm feeling sad
They always try to fill me with glee.
They help me with everyday life
Because they're always there,
I know they love me
And I know they care,
I love my family.

Another type of love is true love
Where a boy loves a girl and a girl loves a boy,
And even if they are shy
They're still full of joy.
And hope their love,
Will never end,
Unless they find a better
Boy or girlfriend.
I love my boyfriend
And I hope our love will never ever end.

Another type of love
Is a love of a thing
All children love toys
Both girls and boys
And there's also a love of a friend
But here my poem has to end.

Abby Foreman (10)
South Farnham Junior School, Farnham

The Nineteen Things About My Cat Rosie

A is for adorable when she comes to my bed and lies fast asleep
B is for beautiful when she grooms herself
C is for clever when she comes to me when I'm sad
D is for daredevil when she goes out to hunt
E is for her eyes which glow in the dark
F is for friendly when she rubs against me
G is for gross when she's eating a mouse
H is for hiss when she sees another cat
I is for I because I'm her best friend
J is for just as she is just and loyal
K is for knowing as she is always knowing
L is for luck as I'm lucky to have my cat
M is for mice when she likes to hunt
N is for no trespassers or she will scratch and bite
O is for omen a sign we will always be together
P is for perfect in every single way
Q is for queen of all the pretty cats
R is for Rosie which is her name
S is for she as she is mine alone and our personalities are
                                                    the same.

Georgia Dawson (10)
Thames Ditton Junior School, Thames Ditton

Limericks

There once was a girl called Louise
Who hated eating cheese.
She went to the shop
And tripped over a pot
And then she banged her knees.

Georgia Imrie (8)
Thames Ditton Junior School, Thames Ditton,

What Have I Done Wrong?

Curled up on the floor I'm left to wonder
Why I am the forgotten friend they never see?
Although like them I often suffer hunger
They ignore me three times a day like I was a tree.

Of course I am the first they call for walking
This they enjoy and also I do too.
But just because I do no talking
Doesn't mean I'm not half as good as you!

All I ever ask for is a pat on the head
And some food when I'm underneath your chair,
But what do I get instead?
Shouted at and treated without care.

Why do I look after your house all day long?
Protecting everything you leave at home.
What on earth have I done wrong?
Why do I always get the moan?

Get out, sit down, to bed and out you go!
I'm fed up being ordered what to do.
You think I want to chase the balls you throw,
But I'd much prefer to chew upon your shoe.

Sam Ridsdale (11)
Thames Ditton Junior School, Thames Ditton

Sunny And Her Bunny

There once was a girl called Sunny,
Who had a rather fluffy white bunny.
It was really nice
But hated the ice
And it cost quite a lot of money.

Dolores Honey (8)
Thames Ditton Junior School, Thames Ditton

Food And Drink

A is for apples that crunch in your mouth.
B is for banana that's slimy and slippery.
C is for crumpets with holes.
D is for duck that's crunchy.
E is for egg that sizzles on the frying pan.
F is for frog's legs that are tasty.
G is for grapes squishy and limy.
H is for ham off the pig.
I is for ice cold as the North Pole.
J is for jam that rhymes with Sam.
K is for ketchup on your chips.
L is for lettuce mean and green.
M is for meat in the oven.
N is for nic-naks nobbly and munchy.
O is for omelette soft and thin.
P is for pasta from Italy.
Q is for Quaker Oats a mushy cereal.
R is for radish a red vegetable.
S is for snails slimy like mussels.
T is for toad in the hole soft and silky.
U is for Irn Bru a fizzy drink.
V is for vanilla ice cream cold.
W is for Weetabix very nutritious.
Y is for the yoke of the egg.
Z is for zested berry very fizzy.

Sam Carvalho (11)
Thames Ditton Junior School, Thames Ditton

A Limerick About A Girl

There once was a girl called Hannah
Who liked to eat a banana
She shared it with her pet
A monkey called Jet
And always played on the piano.

Hannah Mitchell (8)
Thames Ditton Junior School, Thames Ditton

Sad And Lonely

I'm sad and lonely,
I'm stuck in a ditch.
I'm sad and lonely,
Why aren't you here for me?

I'm hurt and in agony,
There's blood everywhere,
I'm hurt and in agony,
I can't move a limb.

Help me! Help me!
Why won't someone help me?
Help me! Help me!
I don't want to die.

My head is pounding,
I'm scratching and scraping.
I'm in a desert,
All I can see is sand.

I see an oasis,
I stumble slowly.
I'm sweltering now,
Oh it's just a mirage.

Hannah Morris
Thames Ditton Junior School, Thames Ditton

A Very Spectacular Place

One day I went up to space
It was a very spectacular place
I had nothing to do
But I was already through
And that's why I tied my lace.

Cassie McCrone (8)
Thames Ditton Junior School, Thames Ditton

Vision Without Sight

The snow falls like the heavens have opened
The leaves fall off the tree and scatter all around
I know the blossom looks lovely and pink falling from the tree
The acorns on the ground, are being carried away by squirrels
The bushes sway in the breeze

I can hear the sound of the wind
I can feel the softness of the grass
I can smell the sweet smell of lavender
I can taste the berries that I picked off the bush
But I can't see

I can hear the sound of the grass swaying
I can feel the roughness of the tree trunk
I can smell the smell of the tulips
I can taste the strawberries
But I can't see

The snow falls like the heavens have opened
The leaves fall off the tree and scatter all around
I know the blossom looks lovely and pink falling from the tree
The acorns on the ground, are being carried away by squirrels
The bushes sway in the breeze
But I can't see.

Katie Channer (11)
Thames Ditton Junior School, Thames Ditton

Limerick

There was a girl called Bevan
Who wanted to go to Heaven
She went on a plane
And got wet in the rain
But went to Severn in Devon.

Stephen Monaghan (8)
Thames Ditton Junior School, Thames Ditton

My Guinea Pigs

I have a guinea pig called Fudge
Who lives with his brother called Smudge
Fudge sits in the cage
While Smudge in a terrible rage
But they also have a fantastic day.

They argue all the time
Which drives me round the bend
However Smudge is a runt
Who likes to hunt
But Fudge is gentle
And loves eating lentils.

They sit on the grass
And bite at the run that is brass
When I first saw them
I felt so mean
So I told my mum that I was keen.

I went to buy them
And got home
Fudge sat on my lap
But gave Smudge a fake slap
As he bit through my arm.

Amy Davies (10)
Thames Ditton Junior School, Thames Ditton

The Zoo

One day I went to the zoo
In year 1982
And went down the stairs
And scared the bears
And jumped in a load of goo!

Emily Hale (7)
Thames Ditton Junior School, Thames Ditton

Christmas

Christmas is a happy season
Everyone gathers around the tree
The happy children jump with joy
It makes them really, really happy.

Christmas is a happy season
Children are happy for more than one present
They are much, much more happier
When they are sure it is Advent.

Christmas is a happy season
The tree is covered in decorations
People share their laughs with others
They then know it's time for celebrations.

Christmas is a happy season
Many adults get out the wine
While many people lie down and look up
And see the stars that shine.

Christmas is a happy season
There is soon a joyful brilliant New Year
Many people stand and count down
Then all the fireworks get to many people's ear
But still they all scream and cheer!

Afshin Zainy (11)
Thames Ditton Junior School, Thames Ditton

Limerick

There once was a girl called Dolly
Who liked to push a trolley
She went to the shop
And then tripped over a mop
And then she blew up a dolly.

Emily Ford (7)
Thames Ditton Junior School, Thames Ditton

The Door

(Inspired by 'The Door' by Miroslav Holub)

Open that door
Where you seek your dream
What you desire is in that room,
Or maybe a stream
Glinting in the moon.

Open that door
Inside is your destiny
Where you'll live for eternity,
Or maybe the scene
That you didn't want to dream.

Open that door
Inside is a wonderful land,
Where there is a playing band
Playing a song,
To cheer you along.

Open that door
Where there is a big, wide ocean
That moves in slow motion
Mysterious and deep,
Where fish do not sleep.

Charlie Takhar (11)
Thames Ditton Junior School, Thames Ditton

James

There once was a boy called James
Who always like playing games
He played squashed banana
And fell into pyjamas
Then he never liked playing games.

Andrew Moore (7)
Thames Ditton Junior School, Thames Ditton

The Horseman

The horseman is coming.
I can hear the clipping and clopping
Of his black horse's hooves.
The moonlight shining on his pistol,
His sword unsheathed,
The whispering voice of the wind in the trees.
He knocks on the inn door and strides magnificently in.
The air is cold,
And a shriek goes up.
As the horseman gallops away,
He sheaths his sword,
And the glint of red,
Catches your eye.
And you see the saddlebags are full.
What has transpired that night,
Will become apparent in the dawn.
Blood flowing from the door
Onto the wet mud,
Is the only evidence the horseman ever existed.
And gold coins,
Pressed into the mud,
Show a trail of death.

Tim Ellis (11)
Thames Ditton Junior School, Thames Ditton

There Once Was A Boy Called James

There once was a boy called James
Who had lots of funny names
Then he decided to change them
When he changed them he paid for them
So he couldn't get anymore names.

Patrick Waters (8)
Thames Ditton Junior School, Thames Ditton

War Worries

You sail across the seas,
You fight, you kill, make war,
You don't want me to worry
But now I'm not so sure.

I hear of all those dead,
And that the war will carry on,
But there are no weapons of mass destruction,
So please now, don't be long.

Please don't hurt the little children
Because I think they do not deserve
To be hurt, injured, or in pain
Just cos soldiers lose their nerve.

I miss you, I miss you,
I know you miss me too,
But think of all those people,
Who miss because of you.

So now, like I said, do not be long
I'll send kisses across the blue,
Until you come back to me,
Until my hope reaches you.

Julia Onken (11)
Thames Ditton Junior School, Thames Ditton

Oliver The Octopus

Oliver the octopus under the sea,
Swimming all around searching for his tea.
Oliver the octopus
Had eight orange wiggly legs
He sees some fish eggs
Under his big head
'Those look yummy and delicious' he said.

Emily White (11)
Thames Ditton Junior School, Thames Ditton

Fifteen Things At The Bottom Of My Bag

Fifteen things at the bottom of my bag!
A pair of smelly gym socks
A fake dog poo
A mouldy house key
A dead rat
My baseball bat
An out of date Twix bar
A pack of pick-and-mix
A dead fish
A broken dish
A feathery hen
My old ink pen
My broken shelf
A picture of myself
An old raw bean
A photograph of the Fulham team.

Ross Bedding (11)
Thames Ditton Junior School, Thames Ditton

Viruses

Viruses are like worms,
Digging in your computer
Each bite,
Each second,
Jams your computer
When the worm's finished eating,
They move to another computer to eat
Crunch, crunch
All they do is munch
Breakfast, worm blast
Lunch, millennium
Dinner, ob-zeus
They are what they produce
Crunch, munch
Watch out, the virus is about!

Nicholas Dossett (11)
Thames Ditton Junior School, Thames Ditton

Fifteen Things At The Bottom Of My Bag

First of all a pencil case
Two football key rings
Number three a shoe lace
Four a dead rat
Five my baseball bat
Then six a box of Twix
Seven a bag of stolen lipsticks
Number eight a piece of my neighbour's gate
Nine a letter for being late
Ten a mouldy sandwich
Eleven my brother's toy bridge
Twelve a fake hand ready to delve
Thirteen my hamster to sell
Fourteen my grandma's black bean
At the bottom of my bag there is my teacher's missing handbag.

Lara Nicholls (11)
Thames Ditton Junior School, Thames Ditton

Golf

On the course with a club
Hole one ends at the pub.
I hit the ball it goes far
I call *'Fore!'*
Down it comes!
It hits Wood's chum!
I start running from the one.
At tee two
It goes quite far,
Hits my favourite yellow car.
As you can see
I'm not that good
I need a lesson from Tiger Woods!

Edward Leithead-Docherty (11)
Thames Ditton Junior School, Thames Ditton

Happiness Is . . .

Happiness is my cat Charlie,
Happiness is koala bears, giant pandas, leopards and dolphins
my favourite animals
Happiness is my fish Snowdrop,
Happiness is pizza, my favourite food,
Happiness is my teddy bear I have had since I was a baby,
Happiness is my best friends Georgia, Laura, Sara and Alison,
Happiness is my trampoline which I spend half my life bouncing on,
Happiness is going rollerblading with my friend Beth,
Happiness is eating sweets while watching TV with Georgia,
Happiness is shopping with my friends,
Happiness is no homework!
Happiness is sleepovers,
Happiness is end of SATs!
Happiness is the summer holidays.

Sarah Kirby (11)
Thames Ditton Junior School, Thames Ditton

Through The Door

Through the wild safari door, see will you
A koala bear and a kangaroo,
Is a magical jungle with tall mossy trees
With a brown cheeky monkey eating the leaves.

Through the dark sinister door lies a headless man
With a small orange pumpkin roaming the land,
And a translucent ghost horse riding around
While the terrified citizens falling to the ground.

Through the beautiful pretty door stands a beautiful house
With a beautiful dog and a beautiful mouse,
With a pretty princess and her beautiful crown
And a beautiful palace and a beautiful town.

Through that door lies a mystery,
And a great big secret, go and see.

Oliver Roche (11)
Thames Ditton Junior School, Thames Ditton

Sixteen Things Under My Bed

A smelly sandwich mouldy and green,
An old pan not being seen,
A missing sock covered in dust,
Two grapes mouldy in crust,
A box of sweets out of date,
A picture of when I was late,
A cosy cat's den,
A leaking pen,
A dog's toy he has tried to bury,
A scrappy carpet which looks like sherry,
Twenty-nine rats running around,
A wobbly book making a sound,
A maths book as old as me,
Got a torch? Because I can't see,
A top I have missed for years,
An old video of Cheers,
Those were sixteen things under my bed.
I'd better go because what my mum had said.

Claire Gibson (10)
Thames Ditton Junior School, Thames Ditton

Happiness Is . . .

Happiness is a time of people relaxing.
Happiness is getting hugged by Mum.
Happiness is stroking a kitty cat.
Happiness is playing.
Happiness is playing football.
Happiness is sleeping.
Happiness is eating and drinking.
Happiness is giving my mum a kiss.
Happiness is riding a bike.
Happiness if having a birthday.
Happiness is having a birthday party.
Happiness is going to Chessington World of Adventures
with Jonathan.

Joel Rust (10)
Thames Ditton Junior School, Thames Ditton

Through That Door

Through that door
Is a deep blue sea,
Where the waves fold for you
To eternity,
As that blue carpet
Rolls for you,
You will see the bareness,
Of that sea which is new.

Through that door
Is a great green field,
Where the sheep dance around
On that shiny green shield,
That wishes green
Makes me keen,
To dance around
Like a bean.

Seren Bresner (10)
Thames Ditton Junior School, Thames Ditton

Tornado

You crept up to my window and blew away my house
You swept away my cattle
And killed a baby mouse
You made my eyes leak
You made my heart pound
You made me feel like
Crumbs
That lay upon
The ground.

Siobhan Byrne (11)
Thames Ditton Junior School, Thames Ditton

Seasons

Winter, winter everywhere
White snow drops, dropping anywhere
You do not know what to wear
So you put on everything you have to wear.

Spring is here
Spring is here
Blossom here
And here over there.

Summer, summer is in the air
So have some fun in the summer fair
You cannot wear what other people wear
So wear what other people could never dare.

Autumn, autumn flowers are dying
But never fear
The seeds are here.

Geraint Thomas (11)
Thames Ditton Junior School, Thames Ditton

Sammy The Shark

Sammy the shark
Under the sea
Searching for his
Tea.

Sammy the shark
Giving a sway gobbling
Up fish for the day.

Sammy the shark
Still eating fish, ah
What a filling dish.

Sammy the shark
Heading for desert
Oh look, it's a sailor's
Shirt!

Jonathan Spence-Bell (10)
Thames Ditton Junior School, Thames Ditton

Through That Door

Through that door
There is a wide open space
No buildings, no houses
Just a wide open space of grass
Where birds sing
And animals roam free
A place where there are no boundaries
And life is not pestered by human creations.

Anthony Ford (12)
Thames Ditton Junior School, Thames Ditton

Mike The Octopus

Mike the marvellous octopus
Was dancing around
Mike's big legs
Could always be found
Swimming and swishing,
About everywhere,
But only huge things
Could give him a scare.

Georgia Hallpike (11)
Thames Ditton Junior School, Thames Ditton

Smart Car Sports

The smart car sports is really cool,
It's shaped like a space pod,
And comes with a pool,
It has its own I-pod
And coats all sorts
I really want a smart car sports.

Charlie Graovac (11)
Thames Ditton Junior School, Thames Ditton

Happiness Is . . .

Happiness is a good thing
Happiness is like when someone gets a ring
Happiness is a whole load of fun
Happiness is like eating a bun
Happiness is like a dream
Happiness is like eating ice cream
Happiness is like diving on the board
Happiness is like buying a skateboard
Happiness is like having a bear
Happiness is like giving a dare
Happiness is love
Happiness is like when you see a dove
Happiness is a bed
Happiness is when someone's not dead.

Alex MacIntrye (10)
Thames Ditton Junior School, Thames Ditton

David Dolphin

David Dolphin likes his pet dogfish doing dances.
David Dolphin likes his dollies.
David Dolphin does deep dives.
David Dolphin takes his pet dogfish to the dogfish doctor's.
David Dolphin likes dancing in the dentist.

Jack Sheppard (8)
Thames Ditton Junior School, Thames Ditton

Hannah The Happy Hamster

Hannah the happy hamster has two best friends.
A horse and a hippo
But at home she is not handful or helpful
Because she always needs help.

Katherine Andrews (7)
Thames Ditton Junior School, Thames Ditton

Italy's Poem

Kitty the kitten likes ketchup
Ellie the elephant likes eating.
Zoë the zebra likes the zoo.
Lily the lion likes lollies.
Millie the monkey likes mustard.
Daisy the dolphin likes dollies.
Sam the snake likes slime.
Harry the hamster likes help.
Dilly the dog likes dummies.
Paris the parrot likes pumpkins.

Italy Wackrill (8)
Thames Ditton Junior School, Thames Ditton

Lovely Lions

Leo is lonely when he isn't in love in London
Lovely ladybird likes to lick lollypops
Lonely lion likes to look at ladies
Lady Louise likes to lick men.
Lemon leopard likes Leo lion.
Lenny loser likes to have lucky lions.
Lizzie lion likes litres.

Maisie Nicholls (7)
Thames Ditton Junior School, Thames Ditton

Animal Poem

Lizzy lizard likes licking lemon lollies.
Tennie tiger likes tickling turquoise tomatoes.
Ellie elephant likes eating eggs.
Rabia rhino loves rice and racing.
Amy anteater ate apples.
Leslie ladybird likes leaves.

Rabia Alichisthy (7)
Thames Ditton Junior School, Thames Ditton

Jungle Poem

Dilly the dolphin dived into the deep.
Tom the tiger is terrific and drinks Tango.
Katie the koala kicks kangaroos.
Rilly the rhino loves red runny ripples.
Lily the lion lives lies.
Dilly the dog is dotty.
Zizzy the zebra zoomed to the zoo.
Dolly the dog is dumb.
Melina the monkey hates marshmallows.
Molly the mouse loves mustard.
Saskia the snake slithers secretly.
Sophie the slug loves the sun.
Francesca the fish flips fast.
Olivia the owl loves olives.

Saskia Clausen (8)
Thames Ditton Junior School, Thames Ditton

The Guy From Ukraine

There was a guy from Ukraine,
Who operated a crane,
He slipped on a ladder,
And burst his bladder,
And now he's in terrible pain.

Alexander Carr (10)
Thames Ditton Junior School, Thames Ditton

My Animal Poem

Lizzy leopard likes jumping.
Terrific tiger likes talking.
Running rhino likes rain.
Anteater likes eating ants.

Nikolai Madsen Boubaki (7)
Thames Ditton Junior School, Thames Ditton

The Cheetah

Waiting in the sweltering heat,
Cautiously listening to the distant patter of feet.
Slowly he lays down a heavy paw,
Stretching out his long sharp claws.

The cheetah hears a nearby bray
And quickly realises it's approaching prey.
Stooping down amazingly low,
He is ready to pounce and raring to go.

Camouflaged by the vast savannah tree,
He reaches out and punctures an antelope's knee.
Red blood spurts from the painful sore,
Leaving the cheetah with a bloodstained jaw.

Once the cheetah is full to the brim
Leaving the carcass of the prey extremely slim.
The cheetah sits up to admire his feast,
To find he is not the only terrifying beast.

The cheetah springs to his velvet feet,
And prudently turns to meet . . .
The most fearful beast,
Who is known as the lion priest.

The cheetah shivers in fear,
As the powerful lion is coming near.
The lion opened his scary jaws,
And stared over at his enemy quivering on the floor.

As the cheetah lets out a fearful cry,
His time of death is surely nigh.

Chloe Walton (11)
Thames Ditton Junior School, Thames Ditton

My Animal

My animal,
Would have the body of a lion,
Soft, smooth, and sleek,
The head of a robin,
With a small beak,
The legs of a zebra,
So it could be really quick,
The tail of a scorpion,
So it could defend with a flick,
The ears of an elephant,
So it could hear very well,
The nose of a hound,
So there's nothing it can't smell!

Or,
It could have the body of a thorny devil,
So nothing could eat him,
The head of a dolphin,
So he wouldn't be dim,
The legs of a rhino,
So that he could charge,
The tail of a rattlesnake,
But make it extra large,
The ears of a cat,
To stroke when it has been good,
The nose of a hedgehog,
For scavenging in the wood.

But as strange as my animal would be,
Would it be any stranger than me?

Daniel Cornwell (11)
Thames Ditton Junior School, Thames Ditton

My Mum Was On A Coffee Break

My mum was on a coffee break drinking milk and tea,
She bought her book and glasses
And began to write about me.

She grabbed some cookies and left them aside,
And flung some flowers just like a bride,
She ran round the corner with her long golden hair,
And ran outside and met me there.

She did not speak or say a word,
For she just stared at a little bird,
She sat down on her wooden chair,
Then I walked home and left her there.

Jessica Hern (10)
Thames Ditton Junior School, Thames Ditton

My Pet Cat

Strolling in the hallway,
Purring out loud,
Waiting to go in my room
To stroll very proud.
Out my room he goes
And into the garden
And sees another cat
So stares at it carefully
Ready to jump
Then our cat purrs
At the other cat
It is very frightened
So it turns away
We give our cat some chicken
To show we are very proud.

Guy Francis (11)
Thames Ditton Junior School, Thames Ditton

Trees

Trees are tall
Trees are small

Trees are thick
Trees are thin

Trees grow tall
Trees grow small

Trees sway left
Trees sway right

Trees are different in many ways
They are different sizes and different colours.

Some grow fruit,
Some grow flowers.

There are so many different types
Of trees like blossom, oak and chestnut.

Poppy Stewart (10)
Thames Ditton Junior School, Thames Ditton

Dinner!

A white necklace glittering in the sunlight,
Nothing has changed on it since last night.

As the spider prepares for dinner,
He comes across another spinner.

They were joined for dinner by a fly,
Who happened to be flying by.

He landed on their fine plate,
Sadly he knew it was too late!

They fairly shared their prey out,
They ate him with a Brussels sprout.

Francis Still (10)
Thames Ditton Junior School, Thames Ditton

The Mind

In the chambers of the mind
You never know what you may find
Maybe it's hot, maybe it's cold
Your mind is something you cannot hold.

In the chambers of the mind
The deep barren wasteland may only hold outlines
Of such memory long forgotten
Because our minds are fragile
And softer than cotton.

In the chambers of the mind
There are objects of every kind,
An ocean strong and a ladder long
A grizzly bear and a flight of stairs
You never know what could be at
The back of your mind for it is something
You cannot find.

Owen Bresner (10)
Thames Ditton Junior School, Thames Ditton

Black White And Grey

Black is a symbol of death
Black is a witch in the night,
Black is the outside universe
Black is the world around me

White is a newborn baby
White is a symbol of joy,
White is the bride on her wedding day
White is the future ahead of me

Grey is the colour of oldness
Grey is a symbol of tiredness,
Grey is a colour we see everywhere
Grey is the past behind me.

Isabel Godfrey (10)
Thames Ditton Junior School, Thames Ditton

Chocolate

Chocolate, chocolate
It is so very yummy
When I feel a crave for it
It always ends up in my tummy.

Chocolate, chocolate
Some types are very crunchy
But every time I eat it
It is so very munchy.

Chocolate, chocolate
It tastes much better than peas
Although peas are healthier
Chocolate will always indulge me.

Chocolate, chocolate
When the word, chocolate is said
I will always scoff it down
And so that I will be fed!

Sara Moon (11)
Thames Ditton Junior School, Thames Ditton

Open That Door

Open that door
What will you see?
Maybe a garden with an apple tree

Open that door
What is your dream?
A forest and countryside with a running stream

Open that door
And what do you seek?
A mountain with snow on its highest peak

Open that door
What is really there?
The real world not a dream.

Aaron Alexander (11)
Thames Ditton Junior School, Thames Ditton

About Bob

There was a man called Bob
Who had a very good job
He got a lot of money
Which he used with honey.

He went to Spain
In a very big plane
When he got there
He pulled his hair
And went very insane.

When he went back home
He went to the Millennium Dome
To find the missing gnome
He looked around him
And then he found him
But then he walked back home.

Kourosh Soheili (11)
Thames Ditton Junior School, Thames Ditton

Nonsense Tongue Twisters

Super Sam the sausage sat sizzling in a pan,
Singing Sue sat sleepily slurping her lamb,
Superstar Cynthia sang sweetly on stage,
Saxon Sabrina escaped from her cage.

Muddled Maddie moaned meaningfully,
Mixed up Mona was made a bully,
Meaningless Margaret manufactured socks,
Manipulated Malcolm managed flocks.

Ruthless Rodger rounds up reindeer,
Ringing Ringo is near,
Responsible Rupert ruined his life,
Reckless Robert married his knife.

Bethany James (11)
Thames Ditton Junior School, Thames Ditton

My Hamster

My hamster Harry,
Is not too short and
Not too long.
His face curls up in
A very cute way.
He comes out at night
And sleeps in the day.
He is still a baby
Because I only got him
This Saturday.
He needs a lot of TLC
And loves to play.
But the best thing of all
About Harry is that he's
Mine and to me only
He belongs.

Alice Pritchard (11)
Thames Ditton Junior School, Thames Ditton

The Storm

The storm swirls across the sky
Rumbling through the village so high
The lightning peeks out from the crags
Destroying all the village's flags

As it crackles through the night
The electric streaks give off light
The powerful energy rumbles up high
Creating natural light in the sky

As it flashes through the air
The lightning swirls in its lair
When it unlashes its mighty power
The village will meet its final hour.

Chris Baller (11)
Thames Ditton Junior School, Thames Ditton

What Would It Be?

What would happen if I opened that door?
What would it look like on the floor?
What exactly would I see?
Something beginning with E or T.
Would it be the sky above?
Or would it be the heart of love?
Would it be the huge deep seas?
Or would it be the bumblebees?
Would it be people kissing?
Or would it be children missing?
Would it be the growing flowers?
Or would it be the huge tall towers?
Would it make me laugh or cry?
Or would it make me kiss the sky?
Would it make me pray to God?
Or would it make me hug Miss Todd?
I really don't know what's behind this door,
But I really do hope that I can
Explore!

Georgia Bixley (11)
Thames Ditton Junior School, Thames Ditton

Through The Door

Through the door you may see,
Flowers, trees, grass, busy bees,
Flowers colourful, grass green,
Trees tall and lush.

Through the door you may see,
Rivers churning, boats twirling on the sea,
Paradise islands, coconut trees,
Wild animals, stripy tigers, roaring lions.

Through the door you may only see,
A garden with grass and a few bees,
A little old pond with paper boats,
But after all it was only a dream.

Bethan Caunt (11)
Thames Ditton Junior School, Thames Ditton

The World

I am on top of the world
My friends are just below me
I am on top of the world
And you are all I see

I am on the bottom of the world
My friends are angry with me
I am on the bottom of the world
And now all you can see is me

I am at the middle of the world
My friends are warm with me
I am at the middle of the world
All my eyes can see are you looking at me

My end is very near
Friends come around me
My end is very near
Then again the world is me.

Nicholas Matthews (11)
Thames Ditton Junior School, Thames Ditton

Leopard

L eaping gracefully to catch its prey
E merging from the dark shadows
O h what a handsome cat
P ouncing silently in the night
A nnouncing its presence with a grunt
R unning swiftly alongside its prey
D eath follows the leopard wherever he goes.

Katja Schlerf (11)
Thames Ditton Junior School, Thames Ditton

People

I do not understand people
They cut down our rainforests
They pollute the air we breathe
So the air is breathable no longer

I do not understand people
They selfishly harm God's creatures
They slay our magnificent animals
For no good reason at all

I do not understand people
They destroy our wonderful world
They poison our rivers
So all the fish must suffer

People have the power
To stop all this harm
For little do they know
They are just hurting themselves.

Charlotte Fraser (11)
Thames Ditton Junior School, Thames Ditton

The Robin

Out in my garden what will I find?
I found a bird of only one kind
A bird so small crouched on her nest
Her black beady eyes watching for pests!
She guarded her eggs, keeping them warm
Till the day they hatched and her young were born.
Then she was busy flying around,
And her mate helped her too scavenging worms from the ground.
Backwards and forwards with food in their beaks,
Worms and insects to feed their chicks.
At last the work's done, they can fly all alone,
They can fly up high to find a home of their own.

Lily Stevenson (11)
Thames Ditton Junior School, Thames Ditton

Hallowe'en Surprise!

Hallowe'en is when things get scary
People dress up becoming ugly and hairy
Cries are heard of 'Trick or treat'
As they greedily gather sweets to eat
Children go from door to door
Filling their bags with more and more
They dress up as ghosts and Dracula
Others wear costumes which are quite spectacular

But when children go to a particular door
They could get more than they bargained for
Because the treats from that hut
Are not ordinary fruit and nut
Just one mouthful and they'll turn green
Their blood will curdle and they'll start to scream

So I remind you on this night
Do not go to this house of fright
So stay at home tucked up in bed
And you'll be safe from the undead.

Adam Jasinski (11)
Thames Ditton Junior School, Thames Ditton

Soaring

Soaring, soaring, through the air!
Soaring, soaring, through the air!

Seeing people as small as ants,
Followed by birds in big, big packs!

Soaring, soaring, through the air!
Soaring, soaring through the air!

See people inside a plane!
Give a wave and soar away!

Soaring, soaring, through the air!
Soaring, soaring, through the air!

Donny Weerasekera (8)
Thames Ditton Junior School, Thames Ditton

My Odd Memory

Today I visited a zoo
No single elephant did a poo
No monkey swung from tree to tree
No honey made from honeybee

But yes there were some weird things
An elephant with bird-like wings
A rhinoceros jumps about
A woolly snake about and out

A stripy cheetah jumps
Sleuths are no longer lazy lumps

At the end I visited a shop
No horse hoof to go clop, clop

Today was odd
It made me sob
A zoo or farm
Not a single barn

This memory will stay with me for long
That's why I wrote this narrative song.

Tom McFarland (11)
Thames Ditton Junior School, Thames Ditton

Numbers Two Ten

One is a coin bronze and round,
Two is a pair of eyes that are brown.
Three for the merrier up and down,
One, two, three up a tree.

Four is a pink or brown bear,
Five is some weird people in a tribe,
Six for a slave sent to pick up sticks
Four, five six, in the hits.

Six seven, eight, nine, and ten
Are for a person whose name is Ben.

Ellie Herrmann (8)
Thames Ditton Junior School, Thames Ditton

The Door
(Inspired by 'The Door' by Miroslav Holub)

If you open the door, there may be
Monkeys, snakes or sharks in the sea.
When you open the door you could also see
Lions, tigers and insects off a tree.

If you open the door, there may be
A garden full of honey from a tree.
When you open the door you could also see
Flowers, trees, insects and bees.

If you open the door, there may be
Rivers, streams, oceans and sea.
When you open the door you could also see
A boat in the sea, sighting a wonderful tree.

If you open the door, there may be
Something more exciting than a tree.
When you open the door you could also see
A mystery, what could you see?

Max Brown (11)
Thames Ditton Junior School, Thames Ditton

Supernatural Goings On

Every night, after the sun has set
An odd thing will come over your pet
Your cats will shiver and your dogs will growl
And inside the woods, something will howl
In the cemetery there is a sudden chill
Nowhere is quiet and still!

Then inside the church the coffins creak
Until they find a victim, they will seek
Out of the night they will come
And if you complain to your mum
She will say 'What's all this nonsense? Go back to bed,
And rest your crazy little head!'

Eleanor Luker (11)
Thames Ditton Junior School, Thames Ditton

The Great Storm

The storm rumbles over,
Its destination reached.
It crackled and belched,
And let loose its anger in a flurry of light.

A sphere of electricity,
Formed at its base.
And the storm rumbled,
And bellowed with all its might.

Lightning crackled down,
But when it hit the ground,
It seemed to sink into,
The sand.

The storm rumbled past,
Its work here done.
It drifted slowly away,
To terrorise another land.

Alex Walton (11)
Thames Ditton Junior School, Thames Ditton

My Pets

My dog is fat,
My dog is good,
My dog is white,
My dog is fluffy.

He loves a juicy, juicy bone
And he is so clever he can use the telephone.

My cat is cute,
My cat is black,
My cat is as good as gold,
My cat is soft.

My cat spends all her time at the telly
And loves a big rub on her belly.

Ellie Gibbs (8)
Thames Ditton Junior School, Thames Ditton

Walk Through The Door

Walk through the door, into your garden,
Sit under the tree and adore,
The tulips in their flowerbeds,
The sun is up on a lovely spring day.

Walk through the door, into your garden,
Sit under the tree and adore,
The sunflowers are standing tall,
The sun is up on a lovely summer day.

Walk through the door, into your garden,
Sit under the tree and adore,
The brownish leaves of summer trees,
The cool breeze on an autumn day.

Walk through the door, into your garden,
Sit under the tree and adore,
The crispy snow beneath your feet,
The snowmen on a cold winter day.

Jake Harris-Wyatt (11)
Thames Ditton Junior School, Thames Ditton

My Grandad

My grandad is so funny
The things he does are mad,
But he often gives me money
So he's really not that bad.

He gets tied up in his dog lead,
He falls into the stream,
His bowls go the wrong way,
But he's number one in the team.

He puts chocolate on his toothbrush,
He forgets to have his tea,
He is a grandad like you have never seen before,
But he's still my grandad!

Alex Bowler (8)
Thames Ditton Junior School, Thames Ditton

What's Outside?

Open the door, what's outside?
You will get a big surprise.
The sea is sparkling over the fence,
Where a fish in the ocean, I can sense.
As the ripples grey and blue,
Sparkling with no telling of flew.

Open the door, what's outside?
You will get a big surprise.
As the bricks crumbling down,
Cars go whizzing across the town.
Everywhere you look, rubbish around,
But what you hear is a terrible sound.

Open the door, what's outside?
You will get a big surprise.
There are fields upon fields all around,
What you hear this time, no deafening sound.
Sheep are grazing here and there,
Where are the cars and sheep, nowhere!

Georgie Morgan Tuffs (11)
Thames Ditton Junior School, Thames Ditton

Frogs

Frogs leaping and jumping.
They jump as high as a kangaroo.
They love eating flies with their huge slimy slippery tongue
And curling them up in his tongue.
Fish like to eat tadpoles.
Frogs stay on leaves so the fish can't eat them.
They jump from leaf to leaf trying to stay away from the fish.
Frogs like to swim to get out of the sun
But when the fish are away too.
Frogs have no tails and have four legs
Two at the back and two at the front.

Angus Watkins (8)
Thames Ditton Junior School, Thames Ditton

Open The Door

(Inspired by 'The Door' by Miroslav Holub)

Open the door,
Into an imaginary world,
Where there are birds and bees,
And a soft, gentle breeze.

Open the door,
Into an imaginary world,
Where the sea floats on the shore,
And there's no rubbish on the floor.

Open the door,
Into an imaginary world,
Where there would be no traffic jams,
And no cons or scams.

Open the door,
Into an imaginary world,
Where there would be no wars,
And people on the streets who are poor.

Open the door,
Into an imaginary world,
Where everything was perfect.

Leilah Nightingale (11)
Thames Ditton Junior School, Thames Ditton

My Nasty And Miserable Life

I have a life as grey as an old fashioned movie,
I go to school just to get beaten up,
I come home in a cast and nine hundred plasters,
I go to bed and have a nightmare all about bloodthirsty vampires,
I am now awake and ready for my ten-thirty duffing up appointment.

Giovanni Cornell-Lombardo (8)
Thames Ditton Junior School, Thames Ditton

Through That Door

Through that door, waiting for you
Is a garden surrounded by trees.
It is silent just for you, and nothing can
Harm you but the sting of bees.

Through that door, bobbing up and down,
Is a magnificent glittering sea
A place where you will never frown
And nobody would there be.

Through that door, rising slowly,
Is a slope with snow,
Where you will never be lonely,
Don't worry listen, I know.

Through that door, you will find many trees standing there,
Standing near as company for you.
Every night they will care.

Through that door, whatever is there,
There will be something, so try,
Through that door.

Jessica Ive (10)
Thames Ditton Junior School, Thames Ditton

Children

Children shout and scream out loud,
Especially noisy ones in a crowd.
They shout and shout all day long.
Their mothers wonder, *oh what is wrong?*

Children!

The mothers don't want their little babies to cry
They want their eyes to be dry.
Mothers say, 'The kids are such a pain'
Then think their tears should go down the drain.

Children!

Melissa Still (8)
Thames Ditton Junior School, Thames Ditton

The Door

Doors can be big,
Doors can be small.
They can't be shaped like a pig,
But can be very tall.

What could be behind it,
Let us go and see.
It could be a bit scary,
Or as happy as can be.

There might be a slimy slug,
Or a stripy cat.
A shiny bug,
Or a big fat rat.

Maybe there will be steps
Going down,
Down,
Down,
Or flies buzzing all around.

I will close the door,
And will open my eyes.
It is nearly dawn,
And the sun shall rise.

Jessica Imrie (11)
Thames Ditton Junior School, Thames Ditton

Wizards

W for wise
I for ingenious
Z for zaps of lightning
A for artistic
R for revising magic
D for dreadful dragons
S for spells
That's wizards!

Max Kingdon (8)
Thames Ditton Junior School, Thames Ditton

My Nana Doddle

I once had a nana called Doddle
And she had a dog called Poddle
She had two friends called Jim and Pam
Who she'd known since she was just a wee lamb
Oh that was my nana Doddle.

Then one day on a long walk
Old Sir Jim saw a hawk
It scared Nana Doddle, so then she fell
And hit her head on a bell
Oh my nana Doddle was out cold on the floor.

Oh Nana Doddle out cold on the floor
And Pam was being such a bore
I said 'OK we'll leave her here
Then come and get her in a year'
So Nana Doddle stayed on the ground

Soon a year came and past
But we'd all forgotten Nana fast
Now if you see her on that hay
You'll probably come to me and say
'Why don't you bring her in?'
I will reply, shouting through a tin
'There she lies and no one cries
Because we've all said our goodbyes.'

Alexandra Manzoni (11)
Thames Ditton Junior School, Thames Ditton

The Big Blue

The water is calm,
There is a light breeze.
The sun shines warm,
Casting a glimmer upon the seas.

The tiny waves,
Clamber up the sandy beach.
Then retreating again,
Back to the deep, blue sea.

But now it is dark,
The air has turned cool.
The waves have grown bigger,
The moon is out full.

Black clouds have now appeared in the sky,
Thunder booms and lightning flashes.
The rain falls heavy,
As the water clashes.

As morning approaches,
The bad weather clears.
A few fluffy clouds travel across the light blue sky,
Whilst in the horizon, the sun appears.

The water is calm,
There is a light breeze.
The sun shines warm,
Casting a glimmer upon the seas.

Joshua Kaplan (10)
Thames Ditton Junior School, Thames Ditton

Keep Your Feet On Firm Ground!

I hopped upon the ship
I loved sailing, hip, hip
The ship was nice and big
Perfect for relaxing like a pig!

Later upon the ship
I decided to take a dip
I jumped off the old ships bark
Only to meet a shark.

It nipped me on my bum
And first missed me on the tum
I called for help and help came
I got hoisted up never to go there again.

Finally when we couldn't see land
I decided to give a helping hand
I climbed the ropes up the mast
Suddenly hearing a great big blast.

Cannon fire, oh goodness me
I felt like doing a great big . . .
I jumped up upon the deck
And saw our parrot going peck, peck, peck

I ran across the deck to an unarmed cannon
And saw our opponent's flag, it was the Baron!
I shot the cannon once then twice
I saw some tails, oh damn those mice.

After a long hard slog we sunk the fools
Thank goodness for our cannons and tools
We sailed home, happy not sad
Those silly enemies were bad, bad, bad!

Conor Hadfield (11)
Thames Ditton Junior School, Thames Ditton

The Battle

The war-horn blows, the trumpets cry,
'Today is a day for men to die.'
The sun still shines in a sky of blue
Watching to see what men will do.

The general shouts; a plan he's made.
The sun's light gleams off his trusty blade.
The troops move forward like a wall of iron,
But in their hearts is a fear of dying.

Over the crest of the hill comes the foe,
The general waits to see where they go.
Clouds of arrows blot out the sun,
Many will die before their work is done.

The lines of troops clash: the real battle's begun,
Only time will tell who will win and who'll run.
The air is rent with cries of pain,
Some men will never see home again.

Blood and gore runs in pools and rivers,
Blades stab hearts, and hack out livers.
Showers of arrows fall like sharp rain,
Adding more men to the heaps of the slain.

Shining swords are sullied with blood,
Glinting armour is covered in mud.
One line begins to break and disengage
Beneath the other's furious rage.

The enemy warriors turn to flee,
The general's fighters have victory.
They shout with relief: the battle is won -
But the real war has only begun.

Louis Morris (11)
Thames Ditton Junior School, Thames Ditton

A Man From Azerbaijan

Once a man from Azerbaijan
Owned a really big farm.
There he had pigs and sheep
But they just liked to go to sleep.

So this man from Azerbaijan
The one who owned that really big farm,
Had a cunning plan up his sleeve
But it blew away in the breeze.

'Oh darn it, flipping heck
How will I pay that stupid cheque?'
Then an idea came to his head
But he was too tired and went to bed.

So the next day after his rest
The man would no longer be second best,
He ran outside in the glorious sun
And ate a very large bun.

He'd rob the bank that's what he'd do
But first he'd have to go to the loo,
He then set off to the bank
Not expecting to see Frank.

He must admit he was afraid
When he saw the fire brigade,
'Give me your money'
But instead they handed him a fluffy bunny.

'Hip, hip hooray' he shouted and then ran
Only to be hit by a frying pan,
The holder was of course Frank
Who practically lived in the bank.

So this ends this funny tale
About a man who had too much ale.

Daniel Pierce (11)
Thames Ditton Junior School, Thames Ditton

Doors Through Life

Doors to places
Doors through stages
Casting a pathway
Through life's pages.

Doors that open
Doors that close
If they reopen,
No one knows.

Doors coming in
Doors going out
What I ask you
Is life about?

Doors for yes
Doors for no
It's hard to choose
Which way to go.

Doors leading here
Doors going there
Passing through a door twice
Would be very rare.

Doors to Heaven
Doors to Hell
Doors to everywhere
Else as well.

Doors for him
Doors for her
Finding the path
That's with you from birth.

Doors and more doors everywhere
Doors can lead you anywhere!

Sam Thomas (11)
Thames Ditton Junior School, Thames Ditton

On The Other Side Of The Door

On the other side of the door
Will it sink right through the floor?
Will it twist and turn or bend?
I wonder what shall happen.

When I stroll through the great door,
Will there be flowers or gruesome gore?
Will it be empty as thin air?
I wonder what shall happen.

If I walk through the old door,
Will it be rain that I see pour?
Will I see anything at all?
I wonder what shall happen.

When you see me open the door,
Will I be trapped for evermore?
Will I come back to see you again?
I wonder what shall happen.

I'm going to go and open the door,
I don't think I can take any more,
But whatever I do see,
Shall remain a mystery.

Sophie Carter (11)
Thames Ditton Junior School, Thames Ditton

Animals

Bears are big and brown,
Purple piranhas are puking around
Tired tigers tripping over
Happy hyenas laughing
Groovy guinea pigs dancing in the moonlight
Fat frogs hopping on lily pads
Enchanted elephants drinking
Ancient apes falling out of trees.

Harvey Brown (8)
Thames Ditton Junior School, Thames Ditton

Open Doors

Open the door,
I'll be here forever more,
I'll be standing just out here,
With a sigh and a tear.

Open the door,
I'm sorry of what I saw,
But now I'm willing to forget.

Open the door,
I am hearing the wind roar,
Warmth is what we need,
I'm withering down to a seed.

Open the door
You're against the law,
I do live here too,
Remember, remember I do!

Olivia Moore (10)
Thames Ditton Junior School, Thames Ditton

Rhinos

Angry rhino,
Strong rhino,
Fussy rhino,
Hungry rhino.

Big rhino,
Bad rhino,
Small rhino,
Good rhino.

Fierce rhino,
Scary rhino,
Slow rhino,
Fast rhino.

Oliver Stephens (7)
Thames Ditton Junior School, Thames Ditton

Monkeys

Down in the jungle you can see
Monkeys swinging from tree to tree,
Climbing up trees and feeling the breeze
Jumping around and touching their knees.

Down in the jungle you can see
The monkeys eating leaves and bees
Crunching and chewing is all you hear
When you're standing so very near.

Down in the jungle you can see
Two little monkeys crawling on their knees,
Now they're running and jumping around
Down on the dark and mysterious ground.

Down in the jungle you can see
All the monkeys are trying to sleep
The fun is coming to an end
But the monkeys are on the mend.

Jessica Merchant (10)
Thames Ditton Junior School, Thames Ditton

Lightning Strike

One stormy night as bright as a light
The lightning struck my house.
It flashed as fast as a bat but nobody every knew.

So here we go, with the flow all up in my bedroom.
But that night again the lightning struck but this time it left something.

The thing was called Ching
It came from the land of lightning.

Ching was cool, but he was cool
And he went to high school.

Natasha Manzoni (8)
Thames Ditton Junior School, Thames Ditton

The Vampire Diaries

Recited in a Vampire accent

Tonight I vake up and see ze stars,
Ze road is calm with not many cars.
I svetch my vings and lick my fangs,
Not a sound of crash nor bangs!

I climb up out of ze vindow and see,
A stving of bats upon ze tree.
I hide avay ven a person approaches
I eat my breakfast blood infested roaches.

I climb up to ze clouds above
Zeze are ze places vich I really love.
Zey are tucked away from ze busy street
And it's ze only place vere I can vest my feet.

Zen I hear something not nice to hear
Ze sound of birds tweeting in my ear
I must hide avay tis nearly light
I shall vake up some other night.

Molly Hills (11)
Thames Ditton Junior School, Thames Ditton

My Hallowe'en

Witches wondering where to go, Hallowe'en, Hallowe'en,
Ghosts pondering around, Hallowe'en, Hallowe'en
Transparent ghosts tiptoe quietly.
Orange peering pumpkins with fierce flicking eyes
Sudden movements petrified people
Once a girl called Mary disappeared!
Blood leaking from people's head, it is real!
Hallowe'en, Hallowe'en, now it's time for cosy bed!
Put my mug on the ledge
See you in the morning
Can't help yawning!

Holly Stanley (8)
Thames Ditton Junior School, Thames Ditton

Through That Door

Through that door,
What can you see?
The birds in the air,
Flying towards me.

Through that door,
What do you hear?
The dog that is silent
Suddenly howling through our ears.

Through that door,
What do you smell?
The flowers in the garden,
Ready to sell.

Through that door,
How do you feel?
Do you feel happy?
Tell me how you feel.

Through that door,
Are your family.
Now I know how you feel,
You feel happy.

Daphne Cheung (11)
Thames Ditton Junior School, Thames Ditton

My Monkey

M agnificent monkey!
O bedient monkey!
N oisy monkey!
K ing of the jungle monkey!
E choing monkey!
Y elling monkey!

Olivia Doyle (8)
Thames Ditton Junior School, Thames Ditton

Snow

The snow will start
But when will it stop

The snow is like a criminal
Covering up all the tracks
Leaving no evidence behind
It jumps from path to path
Trying not to be found

The immaculate clean snow
Looks like a white silk rug
That you could cuddle up to
But in fact deadly when cold

The snow is pursuing animals
Trying to catch them
One by one
It follows them
Speedily trapping them
In amongst the trees and jagged cliffs
The snow will never stop trying to win.

Jonathan Brownlie (11)
Thames Ditton Junior School, Thames Ditton

Dolphin In The Blue

Through the water she comes
She's as shiny as the sun.
It jumps out of the water like a kangaroo,
Then it pounced from side to side.
It's as big as a whale
It hopped out of the water and forced fish to the shore.

Melina Schoenenberger (7)
Thames Ditton Junior School, Thames Ditton

Mr Majeka

Mr Majeka was a very strange man
He killed his enemies with a rather large pan
Crazy he is, you may think
But look into his eyes, you too will like pink.

Now Mr Majeka loved to kill
But only once he had taken his pill
Drugs he was on, for most of his life
But then again, he came from East Fife.

One day he had a clever idea
He made a machine that brewed and sold beer
But this beer is no ordinary drink
It killed his enemies in a click and blink.

He laughed and sniggered through gritted teeth
Now I won't need a poisonous leaf
His enemies died, one by one
At least Majeka was having fun!

One day Majeka came home to his house of pink,
In desperate need of a rather large drink
He found a drink and gulped it down
It was a frothy substance liquid and brown.

Mr Majeka let out a cry of pain
His head was hurting, mostly his brain
'Alas,' he cried 'my end is near
For I have just drunk, my poisonous beer!'

Paul McClean (11)
Thames Ditton Junior School, Thames Ditton

My Friend Is Coming To My House Today

A re you coming to my house today?
B ecause I have got a good game to play.
C an you bring your teddy bear?
D o you want me to do your hair?
E verything we do will be great.
F riends are good but you're my mate.
G ive me a ring to check the time.
H ave you still got that pot of slime?
I hope you'll be able to stay for tea.
J ust all my toys and you and me.
K itKats and cake we'll have to eat.
L ollipops and ice cream for a treat.
M ummy said we can play in the pool.
N ot if it's too cold or it'll be too cool.
O nly an hour before you can come.
P erhaps even sooner I'll ask my mum.
Q uestions and answers we'll have a good chat.
R ight after that we'll play ball and bat.
S o let me know what you think.
T o have a cocktail drink.
U nless you have something better to do.
V entriloquism, video, vaulting or admiring the view.
W ater fights will be great fun.
X ylophones and drums.
Y ou'll have fun, you shall see.
Z oë and all my toys and me.

Zoë Ranger (8)
Thames Ditton Junior School, Thames Ditton

Bangs, Bangs

It sounded like an earthquake,
The rain got quicker and louder.
As the rain took over the sky turned grey,
And the rain kept on falling down.

The rain made big, big puddles,
And made little, little hailstones.
Veerryy ccooolldd water,
Comes out of the sky and makes the grass all soggy.

Lightning going flash, flash,
Cars skidding all around.
Slippery, slidy people falling over,
Everything that was dry now becoming wet.

Thunder, thunder, oh no, oh no
Deafening noises coming out of the sky.
Poor, poor, poor people getting soaking wet
Ha ha, ha ha, the rain has stopped
And everything that is wet becoming dry right now.

Alex Green (8)
Thames Ditton Junior School, Thames Ditton

Mrs Robin

She sings as sweetly as a nightingale.
Flying as smooth as an eagle.
Sitting on her speckled eggs.
Waiting for them to hatch.

Christina Madon (8)
Thames Ditton Junior School, Thames Ditton

Magic

M agnificent scarlet red phoenix
A cid green dragon
G lowing unicorn
I cy white unicorn
C oming by flight over valleys, mountains, rivers and streams
A pair of sapphire eyes belonging to the dragon
L icked by flames is the phoenix.

C runching on bones is the dragon
R unning on steady hooves is the unicorn
E ternally fire loving phoenix
A ce flier is the phoenix
T he fire is hot from the dragon
U nder the volcano lives the dragon
R enewing phoenix
E verlasting unicorn
S oft silky smooth unicorn

Magic is great isn't it?

Tabitha Murray (8)
Thames Ditton Junior School, Thames Ditton

Timmy Tiger

Timmy tiger plays tennis and he's turquoise.
Timmy tiger likes toffee.
Timmy tiger likes tea.
Timmy tiger likes tomatoes.
Timmy tiger watches telly.
Timmy tiger is a Tudor.

Jacob Wallis (8)
Thames Ditton Junior School, Thames Ditton

Animal Friends

A lex is an alien
B en is a bee
C hris is a cat
D onny is a donkey
E llie is an elephant
F reddie is a fish
G race is a grasshopper
H arry is a hedgehog
I ngrid is an iguana
J ames is a jaguar
K atherine is a koala
L ouise is a lima
M ax is a mouse
N orris is a newt
O llie is an octopus
P eter is a parrot
Q uincy is a quail
R udolf is a raccoon
S ara is a snake
T im is a turtle
U na is an unicorn
V ic is a vulture
W ill is a whale
X ercses is an ox
Y ana is a yacht
Z ac is a zebra.

Peter Frame (8)
Thames Ditton Junior School, Thames Ditton

The Leopard

Walking through the wilderness she comes,
Walking with her cubs,
Walking hungry, hungry
Wanting food, wanting water.

At last she sees it,
Food!
A deer drinking from a lake,
Slurping, slurping, gobble, gobble,
Mother warns cubs not to stir,
Off she goes towards the grass right behind the deer
Swift and silent, prowling through the grass,
Stalking her prey
Mother warns cubs not to stay
Cubs do not obey.

Creep, creep forward,
One, two, three, four, five!
Spring!

Grace Evetts (8)
Thames Ditton Junior School, Thames Ditton

Seasons

Spring is here, birds all sing
Now is time to do your thing
Spring cleaning!
Summer is very warm and hot
And mums sit in the sun a lot!
Autumn leaves crisp and red
Falling down onto your head
Snow is falling down and down
And Santa says 'Ho, ho!'
Seasons come and seasons go
Through hot summer sun to cold winter snow.

Kate Mortassagne (9)
The Granville School, Sevenoaks

Summer Holidays

Summer holidays start in our minds,
But we don't start packing 'til the end of July.

Where should we go?
Holland or Congo?
Scotland or Spain?
My dad prefers the rain.

I like relaxing in the sun,
I like a beach offered by my mum.

Town life is what my sister likes
My brother likes surfing and seeing sights.

We figured it out.
We shall go to the Congo.

When we arrive I'm full of delight
And ready to explore.

It feels like paradise over here
I feel like Princess Leah!

A week has past and it's time to go
I am sorry to have to leave Congo.

And now I'm leaving these bright blue skies
But I have to say my last bye-byes!

Amelia Martin-Davies (8)
The Granville School, Sevenoaks

My Cat Tammy

My cat Tammy is very playful and is a tortoiseshell
She loves to sit on the roof and nip your toes.
The annoying thing about her is that in the morning
She comes and bites my nose,
She has a funny sense of humour
She has a brother called Tom.

Laura Morrison (8)
The Granville School, Sevenoaks

The Long Hard Winter

T he long hard winter is normally clear
H olly sprouts everywhere
E ggs don't hatch at all in the winter

L ots of tinsel on the tree
O n the top the star still brightly shines
N o Father Christmas till the dead of night
G ot to get up early to look in my stocking

H ave a lovely Christmas says a Christmas card
A lso there's the new year
R ed-hot fires steam the sky
D ancing and singing all the night

W inter is fun
I t's not very busy
N ever should you mistake winter every year
T urn up the heating just in case
E very year is a brilliant time
R esolutions so your year will be better.

Elizabeth Seeley (9)
The Granville School, Sevenoaks

A Recipe

Five little eggs sitting in a row
Let's get the sugar out and let's have a go.
First pour the sugar in and then the flour.
Let's get the eggs out and have a little power.
Whisk them all round and put them in.
Gas mark five, to cook in the tin.
Let's go outside and read a book
Twenty minutes later I have a little look.
Yum, yum, yum
Lots for tea
None for you
I'll keep them all for me.

Katherine Taylor (9)
The Granville School, Sevenoaks

The Sweet Shop

S taring into the sweet shop
H ow we love it so
E dible cola bottles, liquorice, fudge
R ock, toffee, haribo.
B ody parts and vampire teeth
E yeball gobstoppers for Hallowe'en
T wix, lollies, dolly mixtures

L ight rainbow dust for a fairy queen!
E ndless pick and mix to choose
M ars bars, chocolate mice
O rbit gum, tick tacks
N aughty . . . delicious . . . gone in a trice!
S tarbursts are the best of all
The sight of the sweet shop makes me drool!

Annabel Philip (9)
The Granville School, Sevenoaks

Birthdays

H appy birthday all your friends say
A and hope you have a wonderful day
P resents and cards come for you.
P ackages and parcels are given too.
Y our day should be fun all the way through.

B low out your candles on the cake.
I nvite your friends to celebrate.
R olls and sausages, lots to eat.
T arts and jelly, what a treat!
H ugs and kisses and games to play.
D awn till dusk, what a busy day.
A nother year older, the day is done.
Y ears of parties still to come.

Ciara Dickson (9)
The Granville School, Sevenoaks

The Seaside

The seaside is a place where children play.
The waves lap ashore everyday
Say, did you see that wave?
It crashed right on the bay.
Now it is twelve o'clock should we move to a shady spot?
Should we go here or there?
We saw a spot we sat right on that dot.
We sunbathed for an hour or two.
Then Lucy decided to go to the loo.
When she came back she was bright as rain.
So we sunbathed again.
Jack, Tim, Lucy and I went to sea to scuba-dive.
We saw red fish and pink.
Some with yellow spots and green.
Some with blue stripes and some with white.
After we got on the boat we zoomed back to the moat.
We ran back to our mum and said,
'Can we have a bun instead of bread?'
We munched until lunch was gone.
It was a nice day,
They had time to play when they went home.
You could only hear the waves lapping the shore.

Katie Brown (9)
The Granville School, Sevenoaks

Canada

C anada is an amazing place
A t Algonquin nature park we saw a bear, moose and chipmunks,
N iagara Falls comes rushing down,
A nd there is lots of good food to eat,
D id you know the temperature can get up to 40° there?
A nd every time I go there I have more fun.

Alexandra Conway (9)
The Granville School, Sevenoaks

Graceful Swan

G raceful swan how smoothly it swims.
R aining or not it's ready for spring.
A lthough the night has come it silently swims.

C oming around the river bend.
E ating only grass.
F lowing river carries the swan along.
U ntil a ripple falls upon the water and gets bigger as it widens out.
L ong before moonlight the swan is sleeping with the wind
                                        blowing around.
S hall the swan fly or shall she dance?
W hat is that noise?
A s the swan glides down the river.
N ever will it be known that a swan is gliding it is so quiet and still.

Olivia Haswell (9)
The Granville School, Sevenoaks

Are You My Best Friend?

My best friend is a bundle of fun
I like to play with her in the sun
She makes me happy everyday
And is always there in everyway.

When I'm sad she makes me smile
She'll always go that extra mile
Pulling faces, telling jokes
I laugh so hard I nearly choke!

So each and every single day
We always find a way to play
So now I think you see
Why my best friend means so much to me.

Ella Lane (9)
The Granville School, Sevenoaks

A Walk Through Time

The happiest feelings in my mind made me jump through grass.
The earth was like a dusty desert cracking and splitting through time.
The poached eggs in the sky made my mouth water,
And patchwork quilted fields all around kept me warm all day.
A jungle full of stinging nettles rapidly trapped me in the
                                                        winding path.
Something blue glistens at my feet.
It's an egg, a broken shell.
Did the bird get killed?
Delicious food appeared from rucksacks and drinks were
                                            on the house.
The sun was bright and skies blue with cotton wool clouds.
Full of energy we went on through time.

Elspeth Newey (9)
The Granville School, Sevenoaks

A's Problems

Said A to B 'I'm tired you see,
Of being first in the line.
But if anyone picks a letter
It surely won't be mine.'
The news spread far and wide
And all the letters came to decide
A would have to understand,
He was important also and
A said to Z 'Are you happy?'
'Yes' said Z 'and you should be'
So on that day, A began to say,
'I'm happy, I'm joyful
I'm letter A!'

Isobel Moulder (9)
The Granville School, Sevenoaks

Down At The Bottom Of The Garden

Down at the bottom of the garden
In the middle of the big shady bush.
Where the long grass reaches the tip of the top of the sky
There are three little houses.
In the three houses live
Rainbow, a colourful fairy who is always in a mood to help
Lavender, who is always happy,
And last but not least,
Ruby, a fairy that's always funny.
I know they are there, and if you imagine you can be there with me.

Amelia Wollaston (9)
The Granville School, Sevenoaks

My Special Friend

Bingo is my loving pet,
She always is around me.
She's black and small and very clean,
She would never leave without me.
I cuddle her all day and night
She keeps me safe and warm.
There is no other dog
That could calm me in a storm.

Emily Shepherd-Barron (9)
The Granville School, Sevenoaks

Summer

S o long spring for another year
U npopular winter fades into the past
M y favourite season summer is here.
M any people like summer the best
E quador seems like Alaska compared to this weather
R ounders is the sport for summer.

Flora Donald (8)
The Granville School, Sevenoaks

My Horse

I have a horse her name is Sumi,
She is very bright and never gloomy.
She has three black hooves and one white
But you hardly notice it at night.
She has a very slow walk but a nice fast trot,
I really do like it, I like it a lot.
She has a stable, it is cosy,
When I go in there it makes me dozy!

Alice Paterson (9)
The Granville School, Sevenoaks

Pebbles

P ebbles is my furry friend
E ven though he is small, I love him very much.
B ecause I love him so, he loves me back.
B ut when I have a wound, he licks it for my sake.
L olloping over the grass he goes
E ven I can't catch up with him
S o he is a rabbit!

Venetia Roxburgh (8)
The Granville School, Sevenoaks

The Race

Splash, I'm in the water.
Winning this race is important to me.
I am just behind Leisha the fastest swimmer.
My group cheers me on.
My muscles ache, I find it hard to breathe.
I now have to flip over and do the other length,
This is my chance, go . . .
There's silence and I can't see a thing!

Helena Slater (9)
The Granville School, Sevenoaks

My Special Chocolate Friend

Sadie is my chocolate friend.
She lives with us and loves to play.
Sometimes with her toys, but best of all with us.
Always, full of fun.
Often chasing and swimming too!
A clever friend, she knows when I'm sad,

Or when I'm feeling very bad.
Besides me her friend is food, except onions and tomatoes!
As a chocolate Labrador, she has won no prizes.
But to me she will always come first as my special chocolate friend!

Elizabeth Thompson (9)
The Granville School, Sevenoaks

One, Two, Josh Grew

One, two, Josh grew.
Three, four, dirty floor.
Five, six, clock ticks,
Seven, eight, you're the bait.
Nine, ten, you're not Ben.
Eleven, twelve, what a big belch!
Thirteen, fourteen, go to the haunting,
Fifteen, sixteen, I hate writing.
Seventeen, eighteen, I am hating,
Nineteen, twenty, who are you blaming.

Adam Griffith (8)
Whitstable County Junior School, Whitstable

One, Two, Kiss My Shoe

One, two, kiss my shoe
Three, four, there's a claw
Five, six, there's some lix
Seven, eight, there's a gate
Nine, ten, have a pen
Eleven, twelve, grab my elf
Thirteen, fourteen there's quarantine
Fifteen, sixteen, do some twisting
Seventeen, eighteen, have a mate in
Nineteen, twenty, there's a dragon.

Danny Lindsey (8)
Whitstable County Junior School, Whitstable

One, Two, The Cow Goes Moo

One, two, the cow goes moo
Three, four, sit on the floor
Five, six, get some tree
Seven, eight, get the box
Nine, ten, go to bed
Eleven, twelve, coloured in
Thirteen, fourteen, coloured me
Fifteen, sixteen, I see a dog
Seventeen, eighteen, got me down
Nineteen, twenty, the sun does shine.

Amy Haselup (8)
Whitstable County Junior School, Whitstable

One, Two Sit On My Shoe

One, two, sit on my shoe
Three, four, I fell out the door
Five, six, get the sticks
Seven, eight, get the plates
Nine, ten, get the pen
Eleven, twelve, get the elf
Thirteen, fourteen, break the machine
Fifteen, sixteen, get Dean
Seventeen, eighteen, get the Mate Team
Nineteen, twenty, get the menty.

Andrew Uden (9)
Whitstable County Junior School, Whitstable